WALK THRU the PENTATEUCH

TIMELESS TRUTH
WALK THRU THE BIBLE CLASSIC
LASTING LIFE CHANGE

Discover the first five books of the Old Testament:

Genesis, Exodus, Leviticus, Numbers, Deuteronomy

Dr. Bruce H. Wilkinson

COURSE WORKBOOK

Walk Thru the Pentateuch

Designers: Travis Stoneback, Michael C. Koiner

4201 North Peachtree Road
Atlanta, GA 30341-1207
www.walkthru.org
1.800.361.6131

TABLE OF CONTENTS

DEVOTIONS

TAKE A WALK. CHANGE THE WORLD.

HELPING PEOPLE EVERYWHERE LIVE GOD'S WORD . . . AND LOVE GOD'S WORD.

That's where "igniting passion for God's Word," a phrase we use frequently, comes in. Our mission is to create a path to help people encounter God, to connect them with His heart and open their ears to His voice. We believe that making disciples is more than simply making converts; it's helping people cultivate a dynamic, growing relationship with God. And igniting passion for His Word is a vital part of that mission.

HOW DO WE DO THAT?

By getting people into His Word every way we know how, and with an approach that's engaging, relevant, and memorable—even exciting and fun! In our live events, we race through the Old or New Testament in a few hours. With our devotionals, we linger in the Bible over the course of a year. With our small group resources, we walk through the Bible—actually portions of it or topics from it—in a few weeks. We partner with local churches around the world to provide teaching, tools, and training to pastors, leaders, and all other believers with solid, biblical resources. And over the course of three decades, our discipleship materials have reached millions of people. Walk Thru the Bible ignites passion for God's Word through innovative live events, inspiring biblical resources, and a global impact that changes lives worldwide . . . including yours.

Visit us at www.walkthru.org

STEP INTO THE STORY: INNOVATIVE LIVE EVENTS

Experience live events that unveil God's Word as you've never known it before. Our live events tell God's story in a way that's interactive, relevant, and fun. As you're learning God's story, you're developing insight into yours—and enjoying an adventure that will last a lifetime. We offer more than 10 different live events, including: *Walk Thru the Old Testament* (for adults), *OT Live* (for students), and *Kids in the Book* (for children).

TAKE A WALK: BIBLICAL RESOURCES

Delve into resources that impact your spiritual journey wherever you are. For more than three decades, we have developed resources that help people grow in their relationship with God and apply His Word to daily life. We do that through Bibles, small group studies, devotional magazines, books, and more.

CHANGE THE WORLD: GLOBAL IMPACT

Get involved in a global ministry that impacts lives around the world. Walk Thru the Bible is dedicated to developing a global network of pastors and Christian leaders who make life-changing biblical resources available worldwide. Our global network has helped to change lives, preserve families, address social needs, and inspire churches in more than 100 countries. Reaching their communities in dramatic ways, our global partners are helping to change the world, one person at a time, through the power of God's Word.

Visit us at www.walkthru.org

A WORD FROM WALK THRU THE BIBLE

Walk Thru the Pentateuch is one of our Classic Series DVD studies. Our Classics are those studies that have provided such rich spiritual awareness and deep personal growth that they have remained relevant over the course of time.

Walk Thru the Pentateuch was filmed in 1998, and since then, the series has changed the way thousands of believers understand the Pentateuch. Although the look of the video may be a bit dated, the material is just as relevant and timely today as when the series was first introduced by Bruce Wilkinson, founder of Walk Thru the Bible.

As you walk through the first five books of the Bible, the Pentateuch, you'll discover transformational truths about the God of the Old Testament. You'll discover the tenderness of His affection, the heights of His holiness, and the selflessness of His mercy. You'll discover the God of infinite compassion who pushed the limits of His law to give His children one more chance.

We are honored to bring you this study and pray that you are blessed by your journey.

ABOUT WALK THRU THE BIBLE

Walk Thru the Bible ignites passion for God's Word through innovative live events, inspirational biblical resources, and lasting global impact that changes lives worldwide ... including yours.

Known for innovative methods and high-quality resources, we serve the whole body of Christ across denominational, cultural, and national lines. We partner with the local church worldwide to fulfill its mission, communicating the truths of God's Word in a way that makes the Bible readily accessible to anyone. Through our strong global network, we are strategically positioned to address the church's greatest need: developing mature, committed, and spiritually reproducing believers.

Our live events and small group curricula are taught in more than 45 languages by more than 80,000 people in more than 100 countries. More than 100 million devotionals have been packaged into daily magazines, books, and other publications that reach over five million people each year.

Wherever you are on your journey, we can help.

Visit us at www.walkthru.org

Section 1

Genesis

Genesis is a Greek word meaning "beginning."

Deception. Murder. Terrifying flood waters. Could this possibly be the story of a loving God? Many abandon the Bible because of this apparent contradiction. But a closer look reveals profound logic in these events. In order for man to understand who God is, he must first understand the full picture of who man is.

In Genesis, God spoke the universe into existence. Then He spoke a nation into existence, a nation through whom He would introduce Himself again to a lost world. And through it all, we begin to see a portrait of a passionate God in a relentless pursuit of His relationship with humanity.

Focus	Foundation Events				Foundation People			
Divisions	Creation of the Universe	Fall of Man	Flood of Noah	Tower of Babel	Abraham's Faith	Isaac's Family	Jacob's Conflicts	Joseph's Calamity
	1 2	3 5	6 9	10 11	12 24	25 26	27 36	37 50
Topics	History of the Human Race				History of the Jewish Race			
	Faithlessness of Mankind				Faithfulness of One Man's Family			
Place	Eastward: From Eden to Ur				Westward: From Canaan to Egypt			
Time	2,000+ Years (20% of Genesis)				About 350 Years (80% of Genesis)			

INTRODUCTION

How would you describe Jesus Christ?
How would you describe the God of the Old Testament?

THE 7 VITAL FACTS OF GENESIS

1. Biblically: Genesis purposefully selects events in order to interpret_____.

2. Historically: Genesis begins at creation and ends with the death of_____.

3. Chronologically: Genesis spans a minimum of _____years.

4. Geographically: Genesis moves from Eden to Canaan to_____.

5. Structurally: Genesis is the _____ book of the Bible and precedes Exodus.

6. Descriptively: Genesis means _____.

7. Thematically: Genesis reveals God's mercy in the face of man's _____.

THE CHART OF GENESIS

Part One: 1-11 – Primeval History	Part Two: 12-50 – Patriarchal History
Historical	Biographical
The Human Race	The Hebrew Race

▶ PART ONE: GENESIS 1:1-11:32

THE PRIMEVAL HISTORY

ACT ONE
The choices of _____ and _____ (Genesis 1:1-3:24)

"Of every tree of the garden you may freely eat; but of the tree of the knowledge of good and evil you shall not eat, for in the day that you eat of it you shall surely die." (Genesis 2:16-17)

ACT TWO
The choices of _____ and _____ (Genesis 4:1-4:24)

"Now Adam knew Eve his wife, and she conceived and bore Cain, and said, 'I have acquired a man from the Lord.'" (Genesis 4:1)

"And the Lord respected Abel and his offering, but He did not respect Cain and his offering. And Cain was very angry, and his countenance fell. So the Lord said to Cain, 'Why are you angry? And why has your countenance fallen? If you do well, will you not be accepted? And if you do not do well, sin lies at the door. And its desire is for you, but you should rule over it.'" (Genesis 4:4-7)

ACT THREE
The choices of Seth and the whole _____ (Genesis 4:25-6:7)

"And Adam knew his wife again, and she bore a son and named him Seth, 'For God has appointed another seed for me instead of Abel, whom Cain killed.' … Then men began to call on the name of the LORD." (Genesis 4:25-26)

"Then the LORD saw that the wickedness of man was great in the earth, and that every intent of the thoughts of his heart was only evil continually. And the LORD was sorry that He had made man on the earth, and He was grieved in His heart. So the LORD said, 'I will destroy man whom I have created from the face of the earth, both man and beast, creeping thing and birds of the air, for I am sorry that I have made them.'" (Genesis 6:5-7)

ACT FOUR
The Choices of Noah and the whole _____ (Genesis 6:8-11:32)

"Be fruitful and multiply, and fill the earth." (Genesis 9:1)

"Let us make a name for ourselves, lest we be scattered abroad over the face of the whole earth." (Genesis 11:4)

THE GENESIS APPLICATION

"And the LORD passed before him and proclaimed, 'The LORD, the LORD God, merciful and gracious, longsuffering, and abounding in goodness and truth.'" (Exodus 34:6)

The LORD is _____.

The LORD is _____.

"Let us therefore come boldly to the throne of grace, that we may obtain mercy and find grace to help in time of need." (Hebrews 4:16)

DISCUSSION QUESTIONS

1. Has your understanding of God changed as a result of this lesson? Explain.

_____

_____

_____

_____

2. Why do you think God replaced Abel, the one man who had remained faithful to Him?

_____

_____

_____

_____

3. How did man react to the mercy of God in the book of Genesis?

_____

_____

_____

4. How did God react to the rebellion of man in the book of Genesis?

_____

_____

_____

5. In what ways does your view of God affect the way you live?

_____

_____

_____

6. Name at least one common example of how you sometimes misinterpret God's intentions.

_____

_____

_____

READING ASSIGNMENT

This week, read the first half of Genesis, chapters 1-25.

THE BIBLICAL COVENANT

1. A *covenant* is an agreement or contract.

2. The categories of a covenant:

    A. _____ covenant

    B. _____ covenant

    C. _____ covenant

    D. _____ covenant

3. The conditions of a covenant:

    A. _____ covenant

    B. _____ covenant

THE CHART OF GENESIS

CHAPTER 12:1-3	CHAPTER 12:4-20	CHAPTERS 13-14
Call of Abram in Ur	Travels of Abram in Canaan	Troubles of Abram with Lot
"GET OUT..."	"TO A LAND THAT I WILL SHOW YOU"	

▶ PART TWO: GENESIS 12:1-50:26

THE PATRIARCHAL HISTORY

"Get out of your country, from your family and from your father's house, to a land that I will show you. I will make you a great nation; I will bless you and make your name great; and you shall be a blessing. I will bless those who bless you, and I will curse him who curses you; and in you all the families of the earth shall be blessed." (Genesis 12:1-3)

THE ABRAHAMIC COVENANT:

I will give you a _____.

I will make you a great _____.

I will _____ you and in you all the families of the earth shall be blessed.

"Therefore it will happen, when the Egyptians see you, that they will say, 'This is his wife'; and they will kill me, but they will let you live. Please say you are my sister, that it may be well with me for your sake, and that I may live because of you." (Genesis 12:12-13)

"But the LORD plagued Pharaoh and his house with great plagues because of Sarai, Abram's wife. And Pharaoh called Abram and said, 'What is this you have done to me? Why did you not tell me that she was your wife?'" (Genesis 12:17-18)

THE PROMISE TO ISAAC
"Dwell in this land, and I will be with you and bless you; for to you and your descendants I give all these lands, and I will perform the oath which I swore to Abraham your father." (Genesis 26:3)

THE PROMISE TO JACOB
"Therefore may God give you of the dew of heaven, of the fatness of the earth, and plenty of grain and wine. Let peoples serve you, and nations bow down to you. Be master over your brethren, and let your mother's sons bow down to you. Cursed be everyone who curses you, and blessed be those who bless you!" (Genesis 27:28-29)

THE HOPE OF JOSEPH
"And Joseph said to his brethren, 'I am dying; but God will surely visit you, and bring you out of this land to the land of which He swore to Abraham, to Isaac, and to Jacob.' Then Joseph took an oath from the children of Israel, saying, 'God will surely visit you, and you shall carry up my bones from here.'" (Genesis 50:24-25)

THE GENESIS APPLICATION

"LORD God, what will You give me, seeing I go childless?" (Genesis 15:2)

"Then He brought him outside and said, 'Look now toward heaven, and count the stars if you are able to number them.' And He said to him, 'So shall your descendants be.' And he believed in the LORD, and He accounted it to him for righteousness." (Genesis 15:5-6)

"'LORD God, how shall I know that I will inherit it?' So He said to him, 'Bring Me a three-year-old heifer, a three-year-old female goat, a three-year-old ram, a turtledove, and a young pigeon.' Then he brought all these to Him and cut them in two, down the middle." (Genesis 15:8-10a)

"Now when the sun was going down, a deep sleep fell upon Abram; and behold, horror and great darkness fell upon him. And it came to pass, when the sun went down and it was dark, that behold, there appeared a smoking oven and a burning torch that passed between those pieces. On the same day the LORD made a covenant with Abram, saying: 'To your descendants I have given this land.'" (Genesis 15:12, 17-18)

"Believe on the Lord Jesus Christ, and you will be saved." (Acts 16:31)

DISCUSSION QUESTIONS

1. Why do you think the Old Testament is full of examples of covenants?

_____

_____

_____

2. How would you describe the faithfulness of the patriarchs whom God chose to lead His people?

_____

_____

_____

3. What are some examples of God's promises that pertain specifically to you and your life?

_____

_____

_____

4. Which of God's promises is the hardest for you to believe?

_____

_____

_____

5. Which of the four types of covenants did God use to promise your salvation? Why is this significant?

_____

_____

_____

READING ASSIGNMENT

This week, read the second half of Genesis, chapters 26-50.

Section 2

Exodus

Exodus is a Greek word meaning "exit."

Exodus records the fulfillment of God's promise to Abraham to establish a nation. The circumstances surrounding the early days of this nation leave no doubt that only the all-powerful God could be responsible for their existence.

Focus	SLAVERY		SALVATION				SANCTIFICATION		
Divisions	Birth of Moses	Call of Moses	Conflict with Pharaoh	Exodus from Egypt	Red Sea Crossing	Journey to Sinai	Laws and Ceremonies	Tabernacle Blueprint	Golden Calf	Tabernacle Dedication
	1 2	3 6	7 10	11 12	13 15	16 18	19 24	25 31	32 34	35 40
Topics	Deliverance from Oppression						Preparation for Worship		
	Getting Israel out of Egypt						Getting Egypt out of Israel		
Place	In Egypt		On the March				At Sinai		
Time	430 Years (15% of Exodus)		2 Months (30% of Exodus)				10 Months (55% of Exodus)		

INTRODUCTION

Knowing Exodus
Applying Exodus

THE 7 VITAL FACTS OF EXODUS

1. Biblically: Exodus is the fulfillment of God's promise to Abraham of a _____.

2. Historically: Exodus begins with Israel's bondage in Egypt and ends with Israel's _____ en route to Mount Sinai.

3. Chronologically: Exodus spans approximately _____.

4. Geographically: Exodus moves from Egypt to Mount Sinai.

5. Structurally: Exodus is the _____ book of the Bible and takes place between Genesis and Leviticus.

6. Descriptively: Exodus describes Israel's freedom from Egypt and means the _____.

7. Thematically: Exodus reveals God's redemption and the _____ relationship that He makes with Israel as His holy nation.

THE CHART OF EXODUS

Part One: 1:1-18:27	Part Two: 19:1-40:38
"I bore you on eagles' wings and brought you to Myself." (Exodus 19:4)	
The Reasons to Make the Covenant	Redemption by the Lord

▶ PART ONE: EXODUS 1-18

THE REDEMPTION OF ISRAEL

A. Redemption from Egypt through the _____ (Exodus 1:1-11:10)

"And I have also heard the groaning of the children of Israel whom the Egyptians keep in bondage, and I have remembered My covenant. Therefore say to the children of Israel: 'I am the LORD; I will bring you out from under the burdens of the Egyptians, I will rescue you from their bondage, and I will redeem you with an outstretched arm and with great judgments. I will take you as My people, and I will be your God. Then you shall know that I am the LORD your God who brings you out from under the burdens of the Egyptians.'" (Exodus 6:5-7)

B. Redemption from death through the _____ (Exodus 12:1-13:16)

C. Redemption from destruction through the _____ (Exodus 13:17-15:21)

"But the children of Israel had walked on dry land in the midst of the sea, and the waters were a wall to them on their right hand and on their left. So the LORD saved Israel that day out of the hand of the Egyptians, and Israel saw the Egyptians dead on the seashore. Thus Israel saw the great work which the LORD had done in Egypt; so the people feared the LORD, and believed the LORD and His servant Moses." (Exodus 14:29-31)

"Who is like You, O LORD, among the gods? Who is like You, glorious in holiness, fearful in praises, doing wonders?" (Exodus 15:11)

D. Redemption from the wilderness through God's _____ (Exodus 15:22-18:27)

THE EXODUS APPLICATION

"...He Himself likewise shared in the same, that through death He might destroy him who had the power of death, that is, the devil, and release those who through fear of death were all their lifetime subject to bondage." (Hebrews 2:14-15)

"For indeed Christ, our Passover, was sacrificed for us." (1 Corinthians 5:7)

DISCUSSION QUESTIONS

1. How has your understanding of God changed as a result of this lesson? Explain.

_____

_____

_____

2. In what ways has God "parted the Red Sea" in your life to demonstrate His power available to you?

_____

_____

_____

3. Why do you think God wants you to be aware of His power?

_____

_____

_____

4. Think of a difficult situation you are facing or have faced recently. In what ways might this situation have been allowed by God to reveal His power? Explain.

_____

_____

_____

5. What are some ways you can remember to look for God to show His power next time you face a difficult situation? What difference will this make to you?

_____

_____

_____

READING ASSIGNMENT

This week, read the first half of Exodus, chapters 1-20.

INTRODUCTION

What is meant by the term "Old Testament"?

The Old Testament

1. The two halves of the Bible are named by their _____.

2. The two halves of the Bible are focused on the two different offspring of Abraham—the physical and _____.

3. The old covenant is formally established in Exodus _____.

"You have seen what I did to the Egyptians, and how I bore you on eagles' wings and brought you to Myself. Now therefore, if you will indeed obey My voice and keep My covenant, then you shall be a special treasure to Me above all people; for all the earth is Mine. And you shall be to Me a kingdom of priests and a holy nation." (Exodus 19:4-6)

4. The two conditions of the old covenant:

    A. "If you will obey My _____."

    B. "If you will keep My _____."

5. The three results of the old covenant:

    A. "You shall be a special _____ to Me."

    B. "You shall be to Me a Kingdom of _____."

    C. "You shall be to Me a _____."

THE CHART OF EXODUS

PART ONE: 1:1-18:27	PART TWO: 19:1-40:38
"I bore you on eagles' wings and brought you to Myself." (Exodus 19:4)	
THE REASONS TO MAKE THE COVENANT	REDEMPTION BY THE LORD

▶ PART TWO: EXODUS 19-40

The Relationship through the Covenant

A. The _____ of the covenant (Exodus 19:1-31:18)

"Then he took the Book of the Covenant and read in the hearing of the people. And they said, 'All that the Lord has said we will do, and be obedient.' And Moses took the blood, sprinkled it on the people, and said, 'This is the blood of the covenant which the Lord has made with you according to all these words.'" (Exodus 24:7-8)

B. The _____ against the covenant (Exodus 32:1-33:23)

"And he received the gold from their hand, and he fashioned it with an engraving tool, and made a molded calf. Then they said, 'This is your god, O Israel, that brought you out of the land of Egypt!' ... Then they rose early on the next day...and the people sat down to eat and drink, and rose up to play." (Exodus 32:4, 6)

C. The _____ of the covenant (Exodus 34:1-35)

"Behold, I make a covenant. Before all your people I will do marvels such as have not been done in all the earth, nor in any nation; and all the people among whom you are shall see the work of the Lord. For it is an awesome thing that I will do with you." (Exodus 34:10)

D. The _____ through the covenant (Exodus 35:1-40:30)

"And there I will meet with the children of Israel, and the tabernacle shall be sanctified by My glory....I will dwell among the children of Israel and will be their God. And they shall know that I am the Lord their God, who brought them up out of the land of Egypt, that I may dwell among them. I am the Lord their God." (Exodus 29:43, 45-46)

THE EXODUS APPLICATION

GOD'S MOTIVE IN OUR REDEMPTION

"And I heard a loud voice from heaven saying, 'Behold, the tabernacle of God is with men, and He will dwell with them, and they shall be His people. God Himself will be with them and be their God.'" (Revelation 21:3)

"And the Word became flesh and dwelt among us." (John 1:14)

"Or do you not know that your body is the temple of the Holy Spirit who is in you...?" (1 Corinthians 6:19)

DISCUSSION QUESTIONS

1. Have you ever thought of yourself as a spiritual descendant of Abraham before? How would you describe the significance of this connection?

   _____

   _____

   _____

2. In what ways do you act as God's "priest," bringing people to Him? Give an example.

   _____

   _____

   _____

3. Why do you think God invites us into a covenant relationship with Him, as opposed to forcing it upon us?

   _____

   _____

   _____

4. Has God's interaction in your life ever caused your heart to yearn to follow Him? What happened during this time in your life?

   _____

   _____

   _____

5. Can you name something you've done in the past week that wouldn't have happened if you didn't have a covenant relationship with God? Explain.

   _____

   _____

   _____

READING ASSIGNMENT

This week, read the second half of Exodus, chapters 21-40.

SECTION 3

LEVITICUS

"Leviticus" comes from a Greek title meaning "That which pertains to the Levites."

The measure of God's holiness comes to light through the revelation of His standards for His chosen people. And the concept of a Passover lamb is introduced, spelling out the need for a substitutionary death and foreshadowing the coming of the Lamb of God.

Focus	Worship			Walk				
Divisions	Sweet Savor Sacrifices	Nonsweet Savor Sacrifices	Priestly Role in the Sacrifices	Personal Purity for God's People	Day of Atonement	Distinctiveness in the Nation	Holy Priests and Yearly Feasts	Holiness in the Promised Land
	1 3	4 7	8 10	11 15	16 17	18 20	21 23	24 27
Topics	Sacrifice			Sanctification				
	Access to God			Fellowship with God				
Place	Mount Sinai							
Time	About 1 Month							

INTRODUCTION

The unique purpose of Leviticus

THE 7 VITAL FACTS OF LEVITICUS

1. Biblically: Leviticus was the first book studied by the Jewish child and was the last book studied by the average _____.

2. Historically: Leviticus occurs after the building of the Tabernacle and before the march to the Promised _____.

3. Chronologically: Leviticus spans approximately _____.

4. Geographically: Leviticus takes place at Mount Sinai.

5. Structurally: Leviticus is the _____ book of the Bible and takes place between Exodus and Numbers.

6. Descriptively: Leviticus presents the responsibilities of the priests and _____.

7. Thematically: Leviticus reveals the way to have fellowship with the Lord is through _____
    _____.

THE CHART OF LEVITICUS

Part One: 1-16 – The Way to God	Part Two: 17-27 – The Walk with God
Sacrifice	Sanctification
Day of Atonement	Year of Jubilee

▶ PART ONE: LEVITICUS 1-16

THE WAY TO GOD THROUGH SACRIFICE

A. Sacrifice for the _____ (Leviticus 1:1-7:38)

"If his offering is a burnt sacrifice of the herd, let him offer a male without blemish; he shall offer it of his own free will at the door of the tabernacle of meeting before the LORD." (Leviticus 1:3)

1. "Of your own free _____ "

2. "At the door of the tabernacle before the _____ "

3. "put his hand on the head of the burnt _____ "

"Then he shall put his hand on the head of the burnt offering, and it will be accepted on his behalf to make atonement for him." (Leviticus 1:4)

4. "it will be accepted on his _____ "

5. "to make atonement for _____ "

B. Sacrifice for the _____ (Leviticus 8:1-10:20)

"Then the glory of the LORD appeared to all the people, and fire came out from before the LORD and consumed the burnt offering and the fat on the altar. When all the people saw it, they shouted and fell on their faces." (Leviticus 9:23-24)

   C. Sacrifice for ceremonial _____ (Leviticus 11:1-15:33)

   D. Sacrifice for the _____ (16:1-34)

"Aaron shall lay both his hands on the head of the live goat, confess over it all the iniquities of the children of Israel, and all their transgressions, concerning all their sins, putting them on the head of the goat, and shall send it away into the wilderness by the hand of a suitable man." (Leviticus 16:21)

"This shall be an everlasting statute for you, to make atonement for the children of Israel, for all their sins, once a year." (Leviticus 16:34)

THE LEVITICUS APPLICATION

Propitiation for our sins

"For all have sinned and fall short of the glory of God." (Romans 3:23)

"Being justified freely by His grace through the redemption that is in Christ Jesus." (Romans 3:24)

"Whom God set forth as a propitiation by His blood." (Romans 3:25)

"Believe on the Lord Jesus Christ, and you will be saved." (Acts 16:31)

Three Questions from Leviticus

Have you sinned against God? _____

Do you acknowledge that Jesus is the Son of God? _____

Will you permit Jesus' death to take your place? _____

Signed _____ Date _____

DISCUSSION QUESTIONS

1. Why do you think God required the blood of an animal for atonement of sin?

_____

_____

_____

2. How would you summarize the purpose of the rituals described in Leviticus?

_____

_____

_____

3. Are rituals still common in our culture today? Explain.

_____

_____

_____

4. What are some common ways people try to make up for their sins?

_____

_____

_____

5. Can you describe a time in your life when you've felt freedom from the "ritual" system?

_____

_____

_____

READING ASSIGNMENT

This week, read the first part of Leviticus, chapters 1-16.

INTRODUCTION

"And you shall be holy to Me, for I the LORD am holy, and have separated you from the peoples, that you should be Mine." (Leviticus 20:26)

Biblical Holiness

1. The holiness of _____

"By those who come near Me I must be regarded as holy." (Leviticus 10:3)

2. The holiness of Israel in their separation from other _____

"And you shall be holy to Me, for I the LORD am holy, and have separated you from the peoples, that you should be Mine." (Leviticus 20:26)

3. The holiness of Israel in their moral _____

"Consecrate yourselves therefore, and be holy, for I am the LORD your God. And you shall keep My statutes, and perform them: I am the LORD who sanctifies you." (Leviticus 20:7-8)

4. The holiness of Israel in their use of _____

"And all the tithe of the land, whether of the seed of the land or of the fruit of the tree, is the LORD's. It is holy to the LORD." (Leviticus 27:30)

5. The holiness of Israel in their _____

"You shall therefore distinguish between clean animals and unclean, between unclean birds and clean, and you shall not make yourselves abominable by beast or by bird, or by any kind of living thing that creeps on the ground, which I have separated from you as unclean. And you shall be holy to Me, for I the LORD am holy, and have separated you from the peoples, that you should be Mine." (Leviticus 20:25-26)

    A. Holy in how they _____

"Nor shall a garment of mixed linen and wool come upon you." (Leviticus 19:19)

    B. Holy in how they _____

"You shall not sow your field with mixed seed." (Leviticus 19:19)

    C. Holy in what they _____

CHART OF LEVITICUS

PART ONE: 1-16 – THE WAY TO GOD	PART TWO: 17-27 – THE WALK WITH GOD
Sacrifice	Sanctification
DAY OF ATONEMENT	YEAR OF JUBILEE

▶ PART TWO: LEVITICUS 17-27

THE WALK WITH GOD THROUGH SANCTIFICATION

1. Sanctification of the _____ (Leviticus 17-20)

"You shall therefore keep all My statutes and all My judgments, and perform them, that the land where I am bringing you to dwell may not vomit you out. And you shall not walk in the statutes of the nation which I am casting out before you; for they commit all these things, and therefore I abhor them." (Leviticus 20:22-23)

2. Sanctification of the _____ (Leviticus 21-22)

"Therefore you shall keep My commandments, and perform them: I am the LORD. You shall not profane My holy name, but I will be hallowed among the children of Israel." (Leviticus 22:31-32)

3. Sanctification through the _____ (Leviticus 23-25)

    A. The Sabbath Year

    B. The Year of Jubilee

"That fiftieth year shall be a Jubilee to you; in it you shall neither sow nor reap....Then I will command My blessing on you in the sixth year, and it will bring forth produce enough for three years...." (Leviticus 25:11, 21)

4. Sanctification of the _____ (Leviticus 26-27)

"If you walk in My statutes...then I will give you rain in its season, the land shall yield its produce, and the trees of the field shall yield their fruit...you shall eat your bread to the full, and dwell in your land safely. I will give peace in the land...I will set My tabernacle among you...I will walk among you and be your God, and you shall be My people." (Leviticus 26:3-6, 11, 12)

THE LEVITICUS APPLICATION

"He fell into a trance and saw heaven opened and an object like a great sheet bound at the four corners, descending to him....In it were all kinds of four-footed animals of the earth, wild beasts, creeping things, and birds of the air. And a voice came to him, 'Rise, Peter; kill and eat.' But Peter said, 'Not so, Lord! For I have never eaten anything common or unclean.' And a voice spoke to him again the second time, 'What God has cleansed you must not call common.' This was done three times." (Acts 10:10-16)

"Now the Spirit expressly says that in latter times some will depart from the faith...forbidding to marry, and commanding to abstain from foods which God created to be received with thanksgiving by those who believe and know the truth." (1 Timothy 4:1, 3)

"For every creature of God is good, and nothing is to be refused if it is received with thanksgiving; for it is sanctified by the word of God and prayer." (1 Timothy 4:4-5)

DISCUSSION QUESTIONS

1. Has your understanding of God changed as a result of this lesson? Explain.

_____

_____

_____

2. What do you think of when you think of God's holiness?

_____

_____

_____

3. How does something become "holy"?

_____

_____

_____

4. How does someone become "holy"?

_____

_____

_____

5. What would a Christian need to do today in order for his life to be more holy? If possible, share examples from your own life.

_____

_____

_____

READING ASSIGNMENT

This week, read the last part of Leviticus, chapters 17-27.

SECTION 4

NUMBERS

Numbers comes from the Greek word "Arithmoi" meaning "Numbers."

Perhaps you've heard this phrase in various Christian circles: "All sins are the same to God." Would you agree? It's true that there are no excusable sins. But does God really view all sins the same?

According to the book of Numbers, apparently not. Get ready to find out which sin sent more than 600,000 of God's people into a 40-year nightmare instead of into the Promised Land. And see why their example is such a chilling reminder for us today of the importance of guarding our attitudes toward God.

FOCUS	WALKING			WANDERING			WAITING		
Divisions	Counting and Camping	Cleansing and Congregating	Carping and Complaining	Twelve Spies and Death in the Desert	Aaron and Levites in the Wilderness	Serpent of Brass and Story of Balaam	Second Census and Laws of Israel	Last Days of Moses' Leadership	Sections, Sanctuaries, and Settlements
	1　　4	5　　8	9　　12	13　　16	17　　20	21　　25	26　　30	31　　33	34　　36
Topics	Law and Order			Rebellion and Disorder			New Laws for the New Order		
	Moving Out			Moving On			Moving In		
Place	En Route to Kadesh			En Route Nowhere			En Route to Canaan		
Time	2 Months			38 Years			A Few Months		

INTRODUCTION

A heart-wrenching story

THE 7 VITAL FACTS OF NUMBERS

1. Biblically: Numbers reveals the two-week camping trip that became a 40-year death
    _____.

2. Historically: Numbers occurs after Israel has been spiritually prepared and before they
    militarily entered the Promised _____.

3. Chronologically: Numbers spans approximately _____.

*"According to the number of the days in which you spied out the land, forty days, for each day you shall
bear your guilt one year, namely forty years, and you shall know My rejection." (Numbers 14:34)*

4. Geographically: Numbers starts at Mount Sinai, travels through Kadesh-barnea and the
    wilderness, and ends in _____.

5. Structurally: Numbers resumes the story begun in Genesis and Exodus.

6. Descriptively: Numbers refers to the two times Israel took a _____.

7. Thematically: Numbers presents the tragic story of an entire generation dying in the
    wilderness as a result of their repeated and willful _____.

THE CHART OF NUMBERS

PART ONE: 1-12 THE FIRST GENERATION	PART TWO: 13-19 THE TRAGIC TRANSITION	PART THREE: 20-36 THE SECOND GENERATION
The Preparation of Israel	The Rebellion of Israel	The Re-Preparation of Israel
MOUNT SINAI TO KADESH	KADESH AND WILDERNESS	KADESH TO MOAB

▶ PART ONE: NUMBERS 1:1-12:16

THE PREPARATION OF ISRAEL FOR THE PROMISED LAND

A. The _____ preparation (Numbers 1:1-4:49)

*"Take a census of all the congregation of the children of Israel, by their families, by their fathers' houses,
according to the number of names, every male individually, from twenty years old and above—all who
are able to go to war in Israel...All who were numbered according to their armies of the forces were six
hundred and three thousand five hundred and fifty." (Numbers 1:2-3; 2:32b)*

B. The _____ preparation (Numbers 5:1-10:10)

*"And they kept the Passover on the fourteenth day of the first month, at twilight, in the Wilderness of
Sinai; according to all that the LORD commanded Moses, so the children of Israel did." (Numbers 9:5)*

"So it was, whenever the ark set out, that Moses said: 'Rise up, O LORD! Let Your enemies be scattered, and let those who hate You flee before You.'" (Numbers 10:35)

"And when it rested, he said: 'Return, O LORD, to the many thousands of Israel.'" (Numbers 10:36)

C. The _____ from Mount Sinai to Kadesh-barnea (Numbers 10:11-12:16)

"Now when the people complained, it displeased the LORD; for the LORD heard it, and His anger was aroused. So the fire of the LORD burned among them, and consumed some in the outskirts of the camp." (Numbers 11:1)

"Now the mixed multitude who were among them yielded to intense craving; so the children of Israel also wept again and said: 'Who will give us meat to eat? We remember the fish which we ate freely in Egypt, the cucumbers, the melons, the leeks, the onions, and the garlic; but now our whole being is dried up; there is nothing at all except this manna before our eyes!'" (Numbers 11:4-6)

"Then Moses heard the people weeping throughout their families, everyone at the door of his tent; and the anger of the LORD was greatly aroused; Moses also was displeased." (Numbers 11:10)

"You shall eat, not one day, nor two days, nor five days, nor ten days, nor twenty days, but for a whole month, until it comes out of your nostrils and becomes loathsome to you, because you have despised the LORD who is among you, and have wept before Him, saying, 'Why did we ever come up out of Egypt?'" (Numbers 11:19-20)

"Shall flocks and herds be slaughtered for them, to provide enough for them? Or shall all the fish of the sea be gathered together for them, to provide enough for them?" (Numbers 11:22)

"And the LORD said to Moses, 'Has the LORD's arm been shortened? Now you shall see whether what I say will happen to you or not.'" (Numbers 11:23)

"But while the meat was still between their teeth, before it was chewed, the wrath of the LORD was aroused against the people; and the LORD struck the people with a very great plague." (Numbers 11:33)

"So they said, 'Has the LORD indeed spoken only through Moses? Has He not spoken through us also?' And the LORD heard it. So the anger of the LORD was aroused against them, and He departed...suddenly Miriam became leprous." (Numbers 12:2; 9-10)

THE NUMBERS APPLICATION

"My son, do not despise the chastening of the LORD, nor be discouraged when you are rebuked by Him; For whom the LORD loves He chastens, and scourges every son whom He receives." (Hebrews 12:5-6)

DISCUSSION QUESTIONS

1. What are some examples of the things people say when they murmur against God?

_____

_____

_____

2. Why do you think God takes the sin of murmuring so seriously?

_____

_____

_____

3. Have you ever "murmured" against God about the way He has provided for you? Explain.

_____

_____

_____

4. Have you ever encountered circumstances that could have been the rebuke, chastening, or scourging of the LORD? Describe.

_____

_____

_____

5. What would you have to believe about God not to murmur against Him in your life?

_____

_____

_____

READING ASSIGNMENT

This week, read the first half of Numbers, chapters 1-18.

INTRODUCTION

THE PRINCIPLE OF EXAMPLE:

"Now all these things happened to them as examples, and they were written for our admonition, upon whom the ends of the ages have come. Therefore let him who thinks he stands take heed lest he fall."
(1 Corinthians 10:11-12)

THE CHART OF NUMBERS

PART ONE: 1-12 THE FIRST GENERATION	PART TWO: 13-19 THE TRAGIC TRANSITION	PART THREE: 20-36 THE SECOND GENERATION
The Preparation of Israel	The Rebellion of Israel	The Re-Preparation of Israel
MOUNT SINAI TO KADESH	KADESH AND WILDERNESS	KADESH TO MOAB

▶ PART TWO: NUMBERS 13:1-36:13

THE REBELLION OF ISRAEL

1. The rebellion of the _____ and the nation (Numbers 13-15)

"If only we had died in the land of Egypt! Or if only we had died in this wilderness! Why has the LORD brought us to this land to fall by the sword, that our wives and children should become victims? Would it not be better for us to return to Egypt?" (Numbers 14:2-3)

"'If the LORD delights in us, then He will bring us into this land and give it to us, 'a land which flows with milk and honey.' Only do not rebel against the LORD, nor fear the people of the land, for they are our bread; their protection has departed from them, and the LORD is with us. Do not fear them.' And all the congregation said to stone them with stones." (Numbers 14:8-10)

"Then the LORD said to Moses: 'How long will these people reject Me? And how long will they not believe Me, with all the signs which I have performed among them? I will strike them with the pestilence and disinherit them.'" (Numbers 14:11-12)

"Because all these men who have seen My glory and the signs which I did in Egypt and in the wilderness, and have put Me to the test now these ten times, and have not heeded My voice." (Numbers 14:22)

2. The rebellion of _____ and the 250 leaders (Numbers 16-17)

"You take too much upon yourselves, for all the congregation is holy, every one of them, and the LORD is among them. Why then do you exalt yourselves above the assembly of the LORD?" (Numbers 16:3)

"And the earth opened its mouth and swallowed them...and a fire came out from the LORD and consumed the two hundred and fifty men." (Numbers 16:32, 35)

"On the next day all the congregation of the children of Israel murmured against Moses and Aaron, saying, 'You have killed the people of the Lord.'" (Numbers 16:41)

THE RE-PREPARATION OF ISRAEL

1. The rebellion of _____ (Numbers 20:1-29)

2. The rebellion of the _____ generation (Numbers 21:1-25:18)

"Israel remained in Acacia Grove, and the people began to commit harlotry with the women of Moab. They invited the people to the sacrifices of their gods, and the people ate and bowed down to their gods... and the anger of the Lord was aroused against Israel." (Numbers 25:1-3)

3. The re-preparation of the second generation (Numbers 26:1-36:13)

THE NUMBERS APPLICATION

"Now all these things happened to them as examples...Therefore let him who thinks he stands take heed lest he fall." (1 Corinthians 10:11-12)

"But I discipline my body and bring it into subjection, lest, when I have preached to others, I myself should become disqualified." (1 Corinthians 9:27)

"Moreover, brethren, I do not want you to be unaware that all our fathers were under the cloud, all passed through the sea, all were baptized into Moses in the cloud and in the sea, all ate the same spiritual food, and all drank the same spiritual drink. For they drank of that spiritual Rock that followed them, and that Rock was Christ. But with most of them God was not well pleased, for their bodies were scattered in the wilderness. Now these things became our examples, to the intent that we should not lust after evil things as they also lusted. And do not become idolaters as were some of them. As it is written, 'The people sat down to eat and drink, and rose up to play.' Nor let us commit sexual immorality, as some of them did, and in one day twenty-three thousand fell; nor let us tempt Christ, as some of them also tempted, and were destroyed by serpents; nor complain, as some of them also complained, and were destroyed by the destroyer. Now all these things happened to them as examples, and they were written for our admonition, on whom the ends of the ages have come. Therefore let him who thinks he stands take heed lest he fall." (1 Corinthians 10:1-12)

"For he who eats and drinks in an unworthy manner eats and drinks judgment to himself, not discerning the Lord's body. For this reason many are weak and sick among you, and many sleep." (1 Corinthians 11:29-30)

DISCUSSION QUESTIONS

1. If you had to name one attitude as the most dangerous attitude for the Christian, what would it be? Describe.

_____

_____

_____

2. Why do you suppose people are often blind to their own rebellion?

_____

_____

_____

3. Have you ever seen the consequences of rebellion against God in your own life?

_____

_____

_____

4. In what areas of everyday life are you most likely to think you "stand"? How should you take heed lest you fall?

_____

_____

_____

5. In what areas of life do most Christians rebel against God? Do you believe there are any consequences?

_____

_____

_____

READING ASSIGNMENT

This week, read the second half of Numbers, chapters 19-36.

SECTION 5

DEUTERONOMY

Deuteronomy comes from the Greek title meaning "Second Law."

At one time or another, each of us dreams of leaving behind a great legacy. But what we often overlook is that everyone leaves a legacy—whether planned or not. Some leave a great legacy. And others, well...not so great.

In the book of Deuteronomy, you will see how one man took decisive steps and left a legacy that still continues today. You'll also see how you can apply the same principles to determine the legacy that will be left by your own life.

FOCUS	REMEMBRANCE			REMINDER			REFRAIN	
Divisions	Motives for Obedience	Measures of Obedience	Mentality of Obedience	Ceremonial Regulations	Civil Regulations	Societal Regulations	Commitment to the Covenant	Culmination of Moses' Ministry
	1 4	5 7	8 11	12 16	17 20	21 26	27 30	31 34
Topics	Learning from the Past			Looking to the Future			Legacy of a Leader	
	Israel's History			Israel's Holiness			Israel's Hero	
Place	Moab (East of Jordan)							
Time	About 2 Months							

INTRODUCTION

A Legacy of Wisdom

THE 7 VITAL FACTS OF DEUTERONOMY

1. Biblically: Deuteronomy is the only book Jesus quoted when Satan _____.

2. Historically: Deuteronomy takes place after the wilderness wandering of _____.

3. Chronologically: Deuteronomy spans approximately one or _____.

4. Geographically: Deuteronomy takes place in _____.

5. Structurally: Deuteronomy is Moses' response to the events in Genesis through Numbers.

6. Descriptively: Deuteronomy means the _____.

7. Thematically: Deuteronomy renews the covenant with the second _____.

THE CHART OF DEUTERONOMY

PART ONE: 1:1-4:49 HISTORICAL	PART TWO: 5:1-26:19 LEGAL	PART THREE: 27:1-34:12 PROPHETICAL
What God Has Done for Israel	What God Expects Israel to Do	What God Will Do for Israel
PAST	PRESENT	FUTURE

▶ PART ONE: DEUTERONOMY 1:1-4:49

WHAT GOD HAS DONE FOR ISRAEL

   A. The failure in _____ (Deuteronomy 1:1-46)

"Nevertheless you would not go up, but rebelled against the command of the LORD your God; and you complained in your tents, and said, 'Because the LORD hates us, He has brought us out of the land of Egypt to deliver us into the hand of the Amorites, to destroy us.'...Then I said to you, 'Do not be terrified, or be afraid of them. The LORD your God, who goes before you, He will fight for you, according to all He did for you in Egypt before your eyes, and in the wilderness where you saw how the LORD your God carried you, as a man carries his son, in all the way that you went until you came to this place.' Yet, for all that, you did not believe the LORD your God." (Deuteronomy 1:26-27, 29-32)

   B. The victory in _____ (Deuteronomy 2:1-4:49)

"So it was, when all the men of war had finally perished from among the people, that the LORD spoke to me, saying: 'This day you are to cross over at Ar, the boundary of Moab....Rise, take your journey, and cross over the River...I have given into your hand Sihon the Amorite...begin to possess it, and engage him in battle. This day I will begin to put the dread and fear of you upon the nations under the whole heaven." (Deuteronomy 2:16-18, 24-25)

THE DEUTERONOMY APPLICATION

"My brethren, count it all joy when you fall into various trials, knowing that the testing of your faith produces patience. But let patience have its perfect work, that you may be perfect and complete, lacking nothing." (James 1:2-4)

DISCUSSION QUESTIONS

1. If you could leave your own "Deuteronomy" of advice for your descendants, what would it contain?

_____

_____

_____

2. Why do you think it's so difficult to trust God when our circumstances become difficult?

_____

_____

_____

3. Do you have giants in your past that God has defeated? How does that affect your attitude regarding future obstacles you may face?

_____

_____

_____

4. What parts of your life have been modeled after someone else's legacy? What motivated you to adopt their example?

_____

_____

_____

5. Has there ever been a time when God allowed you to be tested? What was the result of that period of testing?

_____

_____

_____

READING ASSIGNMENT

This week, read the first half of Deuteronomy, chapters 1-17.

INTRODUCTION

Passing on the legacy

"Only take heed to yourself, and diligently keep yourself, lest you forget the things your eyes have seen, and lest they depart from your heart all the days of your life. And teach them to your children and your grandchildren." (Deuteronomy 4:9)

THE CHART OF DEUTERONOMY

PART ONE: 1:1-4:49 HISTORICAL	PART TWO: 5:1-26:19 LEGAL	PART THREE: 27:1-34:12 PROPHETICAL
What God Has Done for Israel	What God Expects Israel to Do	What God Will Do for Israel
PAST	PRESENT	FUTURE

▶ PART TWO: DEUTERONOMY 5:1-34:12

WHAT GOD EXPECTS ISRAEL TO DO

"On this side of the Jordan in the land of Moab, Moses began to explain this law, saying..." (Deuteronomy 1:5)

A. The _____ law (Deuteronomy 5:1-11:32)

"You shall have no other gods before Me. You shall not take the name of the LORD
    your God in vain....
    Honor your father and your mother....
    You shall not murder.
    You shall not commit adultery.
    You shall not steal.
    You shall not bear false witness....
    You shall not covet your neighbor's wife." (Deuteronomy 5:7, 11, 16-21)

B. The _____ law (Deuteronomy 12:1-16:17)

C. The _____ law (Deuteronomy 16:18-26:19)

    1. Laws for the _____

    2. Laws for the _____

"You shall not pervert justice; you shall not show partiality, nor take a bribe, for a bribe blinds the eyes of the wise and twists the words of the righteous. You shall follow what is altogether just, that you may live and inherit the land which the LORD your God is giving you." (Deuteronomy 16:19-20)

"But he shall not multiply horses for himself, nor cause the people to return to Egypt to multiply horses.... Neither shall he multiply wives for himself...nor shall he greatly multiply silver and gold for himself." (Deuteronomy 17:16-17)

"Also it shall be, when he sits on the throne of his kingdom, that he shall write for himself a copy of this law in a book, from the one before the priests, the Levites. And it shall be with him, and he shall read it all the days of his life, that he may learn to fear the LORD his God and be careful to observe all the words of this law and these statutes, that his heart may not be lifted above his brethren, that he may not turn aside from the commandment to the right hand or to the left, and that he may prolong his days in his kingdom, he and his children in the midst of Israel." (Deuteronomy 17:18-20)

WHAT GOD WILL DO FOR ISRAEL

A. The _____ of the covenant (Deuteronomy 27:1-30:20)

"Today you have proclaimed the LORD to be your God, and that you will walk in His ways and keep His statutes, His commandments, and His judgments, and that you will obey His voice. Also today the LORD has proclaimed you to be His special people, just as He has promised you, that you should keep all His commandments, and that He will set you high above all nations which He has made, in praise, in name, and in honor, and that you may be a holy people to the LORD your God, just as He has spoken." (Deuteronomy 26:17-19)

B. The _____ of the covenant leader (Deuteronomy 31:1-34:12)

"This Book of the Law shall not depart from your mouth." (Joshua 1:8a)

THE DEUTERONOMY APPLICATION

"That you may fear the LORD your God, to keep all His statutes and His commandments which I command you, you and your son and your grandson, all the days of your life, and that your days may be prolonged. Therefore hear, O Israel, and be careful to observe it, that it may be well with you, and that you may multiply greatly as the LORD God of your fathers has promised you—'a land flowing with milk and honey.' Hear, O Israel: The LORD our God, the LORD is one!" (Deuteronomy 6:2,4)

"You shall love the LORD your God with all your heart, with all your soul, and with all your strength. And these words which I command you today shall be in your heart. You shall teach them diligently to your children, and shall talk of them when you sit in your house, when you walk by the way, when you lie down, and when you rise up." (Deuteronomy 6:5-7a)

DISCUSSION QUESTIONS

1. Has your conviction to learn God's Word changed as a result of this lesson? Explain.

_____

_____

_____

2. What is the most effective way you know to make sure God's Word is "in your heart"?

_____

_____

_____

3. What things have you done well in passing the baton to your children?

_____

_____

_____

4. What do you consider the most important thing that has been passed down to you?

_____

_____

_____

5. Ten years from now, what will you wish you had done differently in passing on the baton to your children?

_____

_____

_____

READING ASSIGNMENT

This week, read the second half of Deuteronomy, chapters 18-34.

Section 5

Daily Devotions

DAILY DEVOTIONS

Take a step toward lasting life change with these
Daily Devotions. Selected from the pages of Walk Thru the
Bible's *Daily Walk* magazine, these readings will challenge you
to apply the lessons of the Pentateuch to your life. Work through
them at your own pace, take on several in one sitting, or think
through one at a time.

GENESIS 1-2
SIX DAYS OF CREATION

♡ **Heart of The Passage:** Genesis 2:4-25

The creation is both a monument of God's power and a looking glass in which we may see His wisdom.

📖 **Overview**

The first two chapters of the Bible begin at "the beginning." Chapter 1 gives a concise overview of the progress of creation, climaxing in the creation of man. Chapter 2 takes a zoom-lens look at day six. There the details emerge of how God's image-bearers were created—man from the dust of the ground and woman from his rib.

The stage is set, the characters are in place, the drama can begin.

Chapter 1	Chapter 2
Six Days Through a Telescope	Sixth Day Through a Microscope
Creation of the Universe	Creation of Man

🚶 **Your Daily Walk**

"When all else fails, follow the directions." That belated advice is based on a law as universal as gravity—the Law of Design, which states: "Things work well when they function according to the way they were designed; they work poorly (or not at all) when that design is violated." God, the Master Designer, made the water, sky, and land; then He made creatures suited for each environment. So it should not surprise you to discover that birds make terrible submarines, or that fish have trouble climbing trees.

The same design apparent in both the solar system and a desert flower is built into humans and their relationships. The husband is the head of the home; the wife is his helper by design. Violate the design and there's trouble. Follow it and there's harmony and fulfillment.

Grab a sheet of paper and see how many ways you can complete this sentence: "By God's design, I am

_____

_____."

(1-3, good start; 4-7, borderline Bible genius; 8 or more, you must be a design engineer!). If you get stuck, consult Psalm 139:14; 1 Corinthians 11:3; Ephesians 2:10; 5:21–6:9, and Titus 2:14 for some help. With God's help, you can become all you were created to be!

🔍 **Insight:** Big Questions, Big Answers

The first verse in the English Bible uses only 10 words to answer four of the most basic questions thinking individuals ever ask: (1) What is there? (2) How did it get there? (3) Did it have a beginning? (4) What or who is responsible? These answers have been graciously supplied by the only One who was there at the time. (The correct answers are: 1. The heaven and the earth; 2. It was all created; 3. Yes; 4. God.)

ENTRANCE & EXTENT OF SIN

 Heart of The Passage: Genesis 3

The one who falls into sin is a human; the one who grieves at sin is a saint; the one who boasts of sin is a fool.

 ## Overview

The perfect environment into which man was placed is now shattered by the entrance of sin. Satan, posing as the subtle serpent, challenges God's only prohibition on man's use of the garden. Disobedience follows as the first family eats from the forbidden tree and is expelled from the garden. The results of their sin spread quickly as humankind and the whole creation fall under the penalty of death. Cain becomes the first murderer, and the downward spiral continues from Adam to Noah, paving the way for God's sweeping judgment upon the wickedness of the world.

Chapter 3	Chapter 4	Chapter 5
Root of Sin: Adam's Rebellion	Fruit of Sin: Cain's Evil Line	Fruit of Faith: Seth's Godly Line
Entrance of Sin	Extent of Sin	

 ## Your Daily Walk

Has this ever happened to you? You turn on your radio or TV and hear glowing reports of a new "miracle product." Convinced, you go out and buy it, only to discover it fails to live up to its billing. Satan has been in the business of overselling his "product"—sin—for thousands of years. He first tried this approach with Eve in the Garden of Eden. Notice the promise: "In the day you eat of it your eyes will be opened, and you will be like God, knowing good and evil" (3:5). Eve believed his claim and tried his product. The result? Pain, bitter disappointment, and expulsion from the garden.

Where has your resistance to temptation been tested by Satan?

What are some of the false promises he would like you to believe in order to sell you on sin? "If it feels good, it must be right. Everyone else is doing it, so it must be okay. If you haven't tried it, you can't know what you're missing. It won't hurt to do it just once."

When tempted today to fall for one of Satan's false promises, respond instead with this scriptural promise from James 4:7, "Resist the devil and he will flee from you."

Q **Insight:** Same Scheme, Different Results

Compare Genesis 3 with Matthew 4:1-11, and you'll notice an interesting fact. Satan tempted Jesus in the same three ways that he tempted Eve (lust of the flesh, lust of the eyes, and pride of life; I John 2:16). But in Christ's case, Satan failed on every count!

GENESIS 6-9
NOAH'S ARK

♡ **Heart of The Passage:** Genesis 6

It is character rather than separate acts that will be rewarded or punished.

📖 **Overview**

In the course of its rebellion, humanity becomes so sinful that God prepares to execute the death sentence on the entire race. In grace He directs Noah—a just man who walks with God—to build a great ship in order to escape the coming judgment. Noah obeys God, and while the flood waters purge the earth, the ark preserves human and animal life for a fresh start. After a safe landing on Mount Ararat, God gives new directions and makes new commitments to Noah and his descendants: "I will remember My covenant" (9:15).

CHAPTER 6	CHAPTER 7	CHAPTER 8	CHAPTER 9
Preparation for Judgment	Deluge of Judgment	Aftermath of Judgment	Promise of Unrepeated Judgment
BUILDING THE ARK	IN THE ARK	LEAVING THE ARK	

🚶 **Your Daily Walk**

Just imagine: "You say you sometimes get tired of waiting for God to right the wrongs in your day? Maybe you should quit your job and sign on with Noah & Sons Shipbuilders. They're short of help, and you will be doubly welcome if you know anything about building triple-decker cargo ships.

"Seems nobody's ever tried this kind of thing before. But Noah is convinced God told him to do it. Says he's working against a deadline too.

"The contract calls for 120 years—no more, no less. Ol' Noah figures the LORD wants to give people another chance to turn back to Him. God's not in any hurry. That's because He's long-suffering. But the LORD won't wait forever. When the time comes, it's going to get real wet around here. God always keeps His word—and just at the right time too.

"Well, you can start by sawing those gopher logs into planks."

Make a list of the faith-inspired steps that Noah took in chapters 6-9. Noah obeyed God by picking up a hammer and saw. What is God asking you to do to join Noah's faithful ranks?

🔍 **Insight:** When Came the Rainbow?

God decreed the rainbow a tangible sign of His promise never again to destroy the earth by flood. However, Scripture does not indicate whether the rainbow had previously existed, and was then chosen by God as a sign; or whether it was a new phenomenon, suggesting a changed climate after the Flood.

GENESIS 10-11
BABEL & THE SPREAD OF NATIONS

♡ **Heart of The Passage:** Genesis 11:1-9; 27-32

There are no new sins—we just keep rerunning the old ones.

📖 Overview

Chapters 10 and 11 explain the origin of nations after the Flood. Beginning with Noah and his three sons, God repopulates the world. But since the root of sin has not been removed from individuals' hearts, the fruit of sin soon becomes apparent once again in proud, disobedient actions. God deals with human failure by scrambling the languages, causing humanity to disperse over the face of the earth—as God had originally commanded! After describing generations of self-serving humans in general, the narrative shifts to one man in particular—Abram—from whom God will build a new nation.

CHAPTER 10	CHAPTER 11		
Descendants of Japheth—Ham—Shem	Old Problem: Pride	New Problem: Languages	New Focus: Abram
FAMILY TREE OF NOAH	TOWER OF BABEL		

🚶 Your Daily Walk

What's so important about obeying God? He's patient and forgiving. And He will always give you another chance. Right?

Think back over the opening chapters of Genesis. In the Garden of Eden, God gave Adam and Eve a forest of trees to enjoy, and only one tree to avoid. What happened? They ate fruit from the forbidden tree and were promptly evicted.

After the Flood, God gave Noah's descendants one command: "Fill the earth" (9:1). Spread out and repopulate the world. How did they respond? "Let us build ourselves a city, and a tower...lest we be scattered abroad over the face of the whole earth" (11:4). Once again, divine judgment followed disobedience.

God means business when He gives a command. It is not there to be analyzed or debated or disregarded. It is there to be obeyed. Do you believe that? Then complete this sentence: "I will save myself some grief if I obey God today [how?]

_____."

🔍 Insight: 4,000 Years After Babel

How many languages are there in the world today? According to Wycliffe Bible Translators, there are 6900+—only 513 of which have the entire Bible. There are almost 2,000 language groups that don't have a single verse of Scripture available in their languages. Almost 75% of them are located in these three areas: Central Africa and Nigeria, 500+; Mainland and Southeast Asia, 500+; Indonesia and the Pacific Islands, 600+.

DAILY DEVOTIONS

GENESIS 12-14
THE CALL & TRAVELS OF ABRAM

♡ **Heart of The Passage:** Genesis 12:1-9; 13:14-18

It is not enough to want to be a useful tool for God, you must be willing to sit still for the grinding that produces the edge.

📖 Overview

Chapters 12-14 describe God's call of Abram to leave his home in Ur (near the Persian Gulf) and travel to a distant but unspecified new land. Abram faces many potential distractions along the way: the death of his father in Haran, a severe famine, the worldly pursuits of his nephew Lot. But God is looking for a man of faith who will trust Him completely to keep His promises. For Abram and his descendants, those promises include receiving a great name, becoming a great nation, and experiencing great blessing in the face of impossible odds.

Chapter 12:1-3	Chapter 12:4-20	Chapters 13-14
Call of Abram in Ur	Travels of Abram in Canaan	Troubles of Abram with Lot
"Get out…"	"To a land that I will show you"	

🚶 Your Daily Walk

How much room have you allowed in your life for God to redirect your steps? Would you be available to do what Abram did?

Close your eyes and imagine for a moment that you are Abram. God has just told you to pack your belongings and prepare to move. "Move where?" you respond. "To a place I'll show you at the proper time." So you obey. You quit your job, load up your furniture, pack up your family, and head out of town.

Destination: Unknown!

If this sounds farfetched, go back and reread the opening verses of chapter 12, for that is precisely the challenge Abram faced!

What if God should come calling at your house today and say, "Get ready to move!" Or what if He told you to do something else that just didn't fit into your own master plan for your life? Would you be willing to respond by faith and trust Him one step at a time—for finances, a place to live, a new church, a new circle of friends? During a quiet moment today, take a walk and get alone with God. Be candid with Him. If you're available, tell Him so. If you're not but you want to be, tell Him that too. Then relax and let Him lead.

🔍 Insight: Walking in Abram's Sandals.

While Abram's faith was growing, so was his stamina. After walking 600 miles from Ur to Haran, Abram set out at the age of 75 for the land of Canaan—400 miles away. He later made a 400-mile round trip to Egypt for a total of 1,400 miles. Now that's a Daily Walk!

GENESIS 15-17
COVENANT WITH ABRAHAM

♡ Heart of The Passage: Genesis 15

God never promises us an easy time, only a safe arrival.

📖 Overview

Today's reading describes the Abrahamic covenant as it was given, confirmed, and symbolized. God's promises to Abraham are given in great detail, confirmed with a unilateral treaty, repeated, and established by the sign of circumcision. But as the years pass with no evidence of fulfillment, Abraham acts in foolish impatience. The result is a son, Ishmael, who will forever cause the heartbreak of his father, constantly reminding Abraham of the price of his unbelief.

Chapter 15	Chapter 16	Chapter 17:1-21	Chapter 17:22-27
Abrahamic Covenant Given	Abram's Impatience	Abrahamic Covenant Repeated	Abraham's Obedience
Isaac Promised	Ishmael Born	Isaac Promised	Ishmael Blessed

🚶 Your Daily Walk

How would you spend today if you thought you might have no tomorrow? For Abram this was more than an academic question. With his little army of 318 men, he had just thrashed a band of warring kings, rescued his nephew Lot, and brought back the kidnapped people and goods. Now, in the long, lonely night hours that follow, he is scared. Scared that his enemies might return to continue the battle. Scared that his life might be snuffed out while he is yet childless. In his moment of deepest need, with fear eating away at his faith in God, he hears a voice: "Do not be afraid, Abram. I am your Shield" (15:1).

God surrounded Abram with His presence, removed Abram's fears, and confirmed His promise. And Abram "believed in the Lord." What fear paralyzes you most often? Fear of failure? Fear of the unknown? Fear of the past returning to haunt you? Write it down on a large piece of paper, along with the words of Genesis 15:1. Thank God that He can, and will, exchange that fear for His strength and comfort. Then tear that sheet of paper into tiny pieces as you, in an act of faith, give your fear to God and appropriate His peace (Philippians 4:6-7).

🔍 Insight: Hagar's Treatment—Abusive or Acceptable?

After 10 years of fruitless waiting for a son, Sarah offered Abram her personal Egyptian maid, Hagar, hoping to produce a son by her. The Hurrian laws from that period describe this as a customary practice. If a son was born, he was regarded as the wife's. But the painful lesson from Ishmael's birth is clear: God's will done in any way but God's way is not God's will!

DAILY DEVOTIONS

DESTRUCTION OF SODOM

 **Heart of The Passage:** Genesis 18

What could be impossible for the God who created the universe and everything in it?

Overview

Chapters 18-20 relate crises arising in the lives of two of Abraham's family members: his wife, Sarah, and his nephew Lot. Lot's life of compromise and worldly pursuits stands in stark contrast to the life of faith demonstrated by his uncle. In response to Abraham's fervent prayers, God spares Lot while destroying his home town for its wickedness and perversion. And yet, even a man of faith like Abraham can stumble when he takes his eyes off God. On a trip to Gerar, Abraham lies about his beautiful wife, Sarah, calling her his sister in order to save his skin from King Abimelech.

CHAPTER 18	CHAPTER 19	CHAPTER 20
Abraham Prays for Lot	God Destroys Sodom and Gomorrah	Abraham Lies about Sarah
LOT SAVED FROM DESTRUCTION		SARAH SAVED FROM DEFILEMENT

 Your Daily Walk

For the next minute, try to imagine the most difficult miracle God could ever perform. If you were to select the "Miracle of All Time," what would it be? Jot down what comes to mind and, if possible, exchange answers with a friend or family member.

How does your miracle compare with the one described in 18:9-15? God promised Abraham and Sarah a son. At first, that may not appear very spectacular, but consider the obstacles God had to overcome. Abraham was 99 years old at the time, and Sarah was 90. For her whole life, Sarah had never been able to bear children. She was now beyond childbearing years. And yet, even the exact time of conception was pinpointed by God. No wonder God posed the question, "Is anything too hard for the LORD?" (18:14).

If you could ask God for one miracle today, what would it be? Help you overcome a past failure? Conquer a dismal self-image? Rebuild a shattered marriage? Write that miracle in the margin of your Bible next to Genesis 18:14. Then stake your claim daily to the warming truth that God specializes in impossible cases.

Insight: Where Is Sodom Today?

After its destruction by brimstone and fire (19:24-28), Sodom never occurs again in the Bible as an occupied city. Today its location lies somewhere beneath the waters at the southern end of the Dead Sea. A nearby free-standing pinnacle is appropriately named "Lot's Wife."

GENESIS 21-24
ISAAC'S BIRTH; SARAH'S DEATH

♡ **Heart of The Passage:** Genesis 21:1-22:19

Only in obedience can we discover the great joy of the will of God.

📖 **Overview**

The climax of more than 20 faith-stretching years for Abraham and Sarah comes in the birth of Isaac, their miracle son and heir. But soon Abraham's faith is tested again as God calls upon him to sacrifice that treasured son upon an altar. Abraham obeys, showing that the experiences of the past two decades have not been in vain. For his faithfulness to the point of death, God rewards Abraham with further assurances of blessing. In the closing years of Abraham's life, a time saddened by Sarah's death, there remains one important detail: finding a suitable bride for Isaac.

Chapter 21	Chapter 22	Chapter 23	Chapter 24
Isaac's Birth	Isaac's Sacrifice	Sarah's Death	Isaac's Bride
Abraham's Faith Vindicated		Abraham's Faith Verified	

🚶 **Your Daily Walk**

Have you ever wished you had a "timer" that would tell you exactly when God was going to fulfill His promises in your life? A way to tell with assurance when your prayer would be answered for a helpmate, the salvation of a loved one, the end of an extended illness? Abraham must have wished for such a timer on many occasions as he waited year after year for the son God had promised to give him. But in the birth of Isaac God demonstrated that, though His promises may not come speedily, they will come certainly. "At the set time of which God had spoken" (21:2), He fulfilled His long-standing covenant.

It's easy to impose your own preconceived timetable upon God's promises... and difficult to deal with the frustration and anxiety that result when God doesn't answer "on time" according to your expectations. Try this instead: Copy the words of Genesis 21:1-2 onto an index card and place it next to a clock or calendar you glance at regularly. Let it refresh your memory throughout the day that the timing of the Creator of time is always perfect.

🔍 **Insight:** The Issue Was Obedience

God's commands to Abraham to offer Isaac did not mean that God was condoning human sacrifice (a common pagan practice in Abraham's day). Rather, God was testing Abraham's faith in His covenant promises. Check Hebrews 11:17-19 and James 2:21-23 for added insight into this event.

GENESIS 25-26
ISAAC'S FAMILY & WORKS

♡ **Heart of The Passage:** Genesis 25:19-26:5

Learn to put your hand on all spiritual blessings in Christ and say "Mine."

📖 **Overview**

The story of Isaac continues, focusing on his family and work. Though Abraham has died, God's promises to him live on in the persons of his son Isaac and his twin grandsons, Esau and Jacob. Sin, too, lives on—as demonstrated by Jacob's theft of his brother's birthright and by Isaac's imitation of his father's deception. Yet, despite human failings, God's covenant remains sure, as testified in His words to Isaac: "I will perform the oath which I swore to Abraham your father" (26:3).

CHAPTER 25			CHAPTER 26		
Abraham's Death	Jacob's Birth	Esau's Birthright	Isaac the Deceiver	Isaac the Farmer	Isaac the Well Digger
THE FAMILY OF ISAAC			THE WORK OF ISAAC		

🚶 **Your Daily Walk**

"God has no grandchildren." Perhaps you've read that statement on a bumper sticker or poster. It means each generation must be personally related to God by faith. It's not enough that your parents trusted Christ as their Savior; you must make a commitment yourself. Similarly, your children are not saved simply because you are. It is a personal, individual decision. You become a child of God by faith in Christ. So do your children and your grandchildren. Seen that way, it's clear that God has no grandchildren!

And so it is with the promises of God. Each succeeding generation must learn to claim them personally in order to enjoy their benefits. God has promises for you today that Christians have been claiming for centuries.

Check up on your relationship with Christ. Is it strictly firsthand, based on personal faith in Christ's finished work on the cross? Or are you relying on secondhand knowledge from your parents, your church, or your friends to get you through? You can become a child of God right now by believing on His Son (John 1:12). And then you can discover the joy of finding God's timeless promises true in your own life. But the choice is yours. God said, "I will . . ." What do you say? Say it to your heavenly Father right now!

🔍 **Insight:** A Family Tradition

The Cave of Machpelah in Hebron, originally purchased by Abraham from Ephron the Hittite as a tomb for Sarah, would soon become the burial place for Abraham himself (25:9); Isaac, Rebekah, and Leah (49:30-31); and Jacob (50:13).

GENESIS 27-31
JACOB'S BIRTHRIGHT & DREAM

♡ Heart of The Passage: Genesis 27, 29

Waiting for an answer to prayer is often part of the answer.

📖 Overview

Chapters 27-31 introduce the third major character of the patriarchal period: Jacob ("deceiver"), a man who truly lives up to his name! The theft of the family blessing intended for his twin brother, Esau, demonstrates his scheming character. But it is through Jacob that God's promises made more than a century and a half earlier begin to be fulfilled in greater degree. During a 20-year stay in Haran, Jacob works for one wife and gets three more in the bargain, fathers 11 sons and a daughter, and amasses huge quantities of livestock and servants—the nucleus from which God will fashion a new nation.

Chapter 27	Chapter 28	Chapters 29-30	Chapter 31
Jacob's Stolen Blessing	Jacob's Dream	Jacob's Wives and Children	Jacob's Quick Exit
Jacob's Spiritual Life		Jacob's Family Life	

Your Daily Walk

For every Jacob, you'll usually find a Laban. For every individual who insists on doing things his own way, giving God a helping hand, there is often a painful head-on collision with someone who is at least his equal as a schemer.

Laban became God's rod of discipline in Jacob's life. There's no doubt God was accomplishing His purpose with Jacob despite his stubbornness and conniving (28:15), but Jacob could have spared himself 20 years of grief if he had learned to wait on God in Canaan.

Have you noticed "The Laban Principle" at work in your own spiritual life? God's stroke of discipline may be applied by a family member, a fellow employee, a creditor. But the goal is always the same: to help you develop spiritual maturity.

Write out a one-paragraph description of exactly what you are going to do the next time you feel like rushing ahead of God. Chances are, before the week is out you'll need it . . . and use it!

🔍 Insight: Marital Bliss . . . or Marital Blisters?

The wisdom of God's original one man/one woman blueprint for marriage is illustrated in the sad example of Jacob's household, where jealousy, bickering, and scheming between Leah and Rachel were regular occurrences. Refresh your memory of family life God's way by rereading Genesis 2:23-24. Then look up 1 Kings 11:1-8 to discover another man for whom multiple wives meant multiplied woes.

GENESIS 32-36
STRUGGLES OF JACOB & ESAU

 **Heart of The Passage:** Genesis 32

A steward is one who owns nothing, yet is responsible for caring for everything.

Overview

In chapters 32-36, Jacob the schemer becomes Jacob the servant of God. After leaving his Uncle Laban, Jacob fears the inevitable reunion with his estranged brother, Esau. But before he can be reconciled to Esau, he must first be reconciled to God. At the Jabbok River he wrestles with the angel of the Lord, insisting on a blessing before he will release him. The angel assures him of God's continued presence, and leaves him with a new name (Israel, "God strives") and a permanent limp. After an emotional reunion with Esau, Jacob returns to Canaan, where God confirms His promises to Abraham and Isaac—promises of a large posterity and a new homeland.

Chapter 32	Chapter 33	Chapter 34	Chapters 35-36
Jacob's Encounter with an Angel	Jacob's Encounter with Esau	Dinah's Encounter with Shechem	Jacob's Encounter with God
Jacob Struggles with Esau		Jacob's Family Struggles	

Your Daily Walk

Is it possible to be a rich Christian in the will of God? That question would have brought a chuckle from Abraham or Jacob. Both men were fabulously wealthy in their day. Jacob in particular shows how a person, blessed by God, can gain great amounts of earthly goods. His own personal testimony is found in 32:10: "I am not worthy of the least of all the mercies and of all the truth which You have shown Your servant; for I crossed over this Jordan with my staff, and now I have become two companies."

When he first crossed the Jordan, all Jacob owned was the staff in his hand and the clothes on his back. Now, some 20 years later, it takes two companies of men to carry all of God's blessings back across.

Reflect on the material possessions God has given you. Could it be that God has prospered you so that you in turn might be a blessing to others? And if so, who are the "others" God has brought into your life for that purpose? If God brings someone to mind, write that individual's name in the margin. Then let Jesus' own words in Acts 20:35 spur you to action today!

Insight: When God Prospers Someone, Look Out!

Beginning with nothing, Jacob amassed such wealth over 20 years that when he left for Canaan he could afford a gift of 580 animals to his brother, Esau, without straining the family budget!

GENESIS 37-40
JOSEPH'S ENSLAVEMENT

 **Heart of The Passage:** Genesis 37-39

The best of saints have borne the worst of sufferings.

📖 Overview

Beginning with chapter 37, the narrative focuses on the next generation: Joseph, dreamer of dreams. Though he is the favorite son of his father, Jacob, Joseph alienates himself from his brothers by his forthrightness. Envy grows into hatred, until finally the brothers sell him into slavery. Taken to Egypt, Joseph continues to suffer injustices, first at the hands of Potiphar's wife, and later from the forgetful chief butler. While Joseph is resisting the temptation of immorality, his brother Judah falls prey to the same sin. Clearly something is needed to insulate the chosen family from moral corruption for the next four centuries while it multiplies into a mighty nation.

Chapter 37	Chapter 38	Chapter 39	Chapter 40
Joseph Sold	Judah Shamed	Joseph Framed	Joseph Forgotten
Beloved Son in Canaan		Trusted Steward in Egypt	

🚶 Your Daily Walk

"I know some of the things I do to be accepted by my friends are wrong. But if I don't go along, they'll laugh at me!"

Joseph could relate to that statement. He learned firsthand the consequences of doing what was right. He could have avoided much discomfort by deciding to disobey his father or give into Mrs. Potiphar. Loyalty to his convictions carried a price tag.

But faithfulness had its compensations too. Note the repeated expression in chapter 39: "The LORD was with Joseph." Now, which would you rather be: a guilt-ridden brother trying to explain Joseph's disappearance, Judah trying to untangle the mess created by his lack of restraint, Potiphar's frustrated wife, or Joseph? Only one of these individuals was truly free.

Where is compromise threatening to dull the cutting edge of your faith? Ask God to give you the courage to stand true to Him with love and tact. Then take the next opportunity to set the record straight and make your convictions known to all parties involved.

🔍 Insight: Clothes Mark the Man

Joseph's famous "coat of many colors" was probably an ornamented, ankle-length coat with long sleeves. It identified the wearer as a favorite son and perhaps indicated Jacob's intent to make Joseph chief heir of the family fortune.

GENESIS 41-44
JOSEPH'S EGYPTIAN RULE

♡ **Heart of The Passage:** Genesis 43-44

Sins concealed by man are never canceled by God.

📖 **Overview**

A difficult dream sent by God to Pharaoh jars the memory of the chief butler, and Joseph is promoted from prisoner to prime minister because of his God-given insight. The dream is a reliable forecast of the prosperity and famine in the years ahead. The worldwide famine prompts Jacob to send 10 sons to Egypt for grain, where Joseph, recognizing them immediately, proceeds to teach them a painful lesson. A series of confrontations builds up to the climax in chapter 44, where the brothers unknowingly fulfill the boyhood dreams of Joseph.

CHAPTER 41		CHAPTER 42	CHAPTER 43	CHAPTER 44
Pharaoh's Vision	Joseph's Vindication	Brothers' Visit	Benjamin's Visit	Joseph's Vengeance
JOSEPH EXALTED FROM PRISON		BROTHERS HUMBLED IN THE PALACE		

 Your Daily Walk

There has yet to be a truly "secret sin." For years, Joseph's brothers had lived with their cunning deception of Jacob. The secret was so complete that Jacob probably blamed himself for the loss of his favorite son. And the other sons, though seeing the agony of soul experienced by their father, maintained their conspiracy of silence at his expense.

But they overlooked one witness to their crime—God. As Judah discovered, "God has found out the iniquity of your servants" (44:16). God gave them time to set things right on their own. Then He applied pressure. The result was a band of frightened men who seemed to be haunted by the memory of their lost brother. Guilt, anxiety, and uncertainty were their constant companions until their wrong was set right through confession and restoration.

As a sinner in the presence of God, you have two choices. You can carry the anxiety of your "secret" sins until God chooses to expose them. Or you can confess those sins to God and to those you've wronged, and as a result find forgiveness and peace. Because of Christ's death, you can take steps today to make things right with a brother or sister, pastor or neighbor, spouse or roommate. Will you do it?

🔍 **Insight:** Whatever Happened to the Tribe of Joseph?

Joseph's sons, Manasseh and Ephraim, were later "adopted" by Jacob (48:5). Consequently, the descendants of Joseph would later comprise two tribes of Israel, named respectively for his two sons.

JOSEPH'S FAMILY HONORED

♡ Heart of The Passage: Genesis 47

When God measures the greatness of an individual, He puts the tape measure around the heart, not the head.

📖 Overview

Joseph, no longer able to maintain the masquerade, reveals his true identity to his terrified brothers. His explanation of recent events (45:5-8) reveals the spiritual perspective that sustained him through years of heartache and uncertainty. In keeping with the prophecy given to Abram (15:13), God assures Jacob that a sojourn in Egypt is divinely approved. And so the entire Jewish population (70 in number) moves to Goshen, which will become home for the fledgling nation for the next 400 years.

CHAPTER 45	CHAPTER 46	CHAPTER 47
Joseph's Secret	Jacob's Sojourn	Jacob's Satisfaction
A BROTHER RESURRECTED	A FAMILY REUNITED	A FATHER REWARDED

🚶 Your Daily Walk

The contrast must have been striking. Into the court of the most powerful king on earth hobbled an old man dressed in the rough garb of a Bedouin tent dweller. Pharaoh was granting an audience to Jacob out of respect for Joseph.

And Jacob, the seemingly insignificant old man, blessed the king (47:7-10)!

Pharaoh didn't know it, but he was being blessed by none other than Israel, the Prince of God. For all his supposed importance, Pharaoh would subsequently fade into oblivion. Even his name would disappear from historical records. Yet this old shepherd would continue to occupy a place of honor throughout the centuries. God's people would be called the "children of Israel," and God would identify Himself henceforth as "the God of Jacob." From Jacob's line would come the King of Kings, who "shall reign over the house of Jacob forever."

Appearances can be deceiving. You, like Jacob, may not look like a VIP in the eyes of the world. But you are. Your importance, like Jacob's, does not stem from what you have made of yourself, but what Christ has made of you. On a sheet of paper, see if you can complete this sentence 10 ways: "Because I am a child of God, I am _____." Then live out your identity today as a child of the King!

🔍 Insight: "You Did It. . . He Did It!"

The words "You sold me . . . God sent me" (45:5) form a classic statement of God's providence. Looking backward, Joseph could clearly see both elements—human and divine—at work in God's plan.

DAILY DEVOTIONS

GENESIS 48-50
FINAL DAYS OF JACOB

♡ Heart of The Passage: Genesis 50

All Christ's blessings are like Him: spiritual and heavenly.

📖 Overview

Chapters 48-50 conclude the book of Genesis by recording the final acts of Jacob and Joseph, along with their deaths and burials. Jacob's blessing upon Joseph's two sons, announcing that the younger would be more honored than the older, is in keeping with the pattern established in Genesis (Isaac instead of Ishmael, Jacob instead of Esau, Joseph instead of Reuben). As his final earthly act, Jacob blesses each of his 12 sons, giving a divinely guided pronouncement of their future history. Jacob's body is embalmed and taken back to Canaan for burial, and when Joseph dies, his body remains in Egypt until the release of the newly born nation of Israel.

Chapter 48	Chapter 49	Chapter 50:1-21	Chapter 50:22-26
Joseph's Sons Blessed	Jacob's Sons Blessed	Jacob's Death and Burial	Joseph's Death
Jacob's Last Days		Joseph's Last Days	

🚶 Your Daily Walk

Do you sometimes wish your life could count more for God...that you could have more of an impact for good in the lives of those around you? You plod along faithfully, but nothing much ever seems to come of it. In fact, you're tempted to throw in the spiritual towel.

God's plan is larger than any one person. In an amazing way He weaves together the lives of many different people to accomplish His will. Joseph is a good example. Torn from his family, ill-treated and imprisoned, he later emerges as ruler in Egypt. And why? "God meant it for good, in order to bring it about as it is this day, to save many people alive" (50:20). Joseph's family and the entire nation of Egypt soon owed their survival to Joseph's leadership.

How many lives do you touch every day? Make a mental list. The number might surprise you! Your spouse, your parents, the kids, the boss, the teacher. Don't forget the neighbors, the people in your office, the mail carrier, the cashier.

Select one name and one way God could use you to touch that life with a smile, a kind word, a thoughtful act. Then allow God to use you today—for good.

🔍 Insight: Egyptian Mortuary Service

Embalming usually took 40 days and was available in several different price ranges. When completed, the coffin was left standing upright against the wall of the burial chamber.

♡ **Heart of The Passage:** Exodus 1:8-2:10

Patience is a virtue that carries a lot of wait!

📖 Overview

As Jacob's descendants continue to multiply and prosper in Goshen, they pose a growing threat to the new Egyptian ruler. His plan to kill all newborn Hebrew boys is thwarted by the courageous midwives, and in this context of danger the child Moses is born. Destined to become the deliverer of God's people, Moses enjoys the finest of education in Pharaoh's court. But when he seeks to deliver Israel in his own time and way, Moses finds himself fleeing for his life to the desert of Midian. There he spends the next 40 years tending sheep and awaiting God's instructions for freeing His people.

CHAPTER 1		CHAPTER 2	
Israel's Growth in Egypt	Israel's Groaning in Egypt	Moses' Birth in Egypt	Moses' Training in Midian
EGYPT THE OPPRESSOR		MOSES THE DELIVERER	

🚶 Your Daily Walk

Where are you currently enrolled in God's "School of Patience"? Put a check next to the "classroom" where you are learning the most right now about bearing up under difficult circumstances:

☐ Home   ☐ School   ☐ Work   ☐ Church   ☐ Marriage   ☐ Hospital

Moses learned patience in the desert as he tended sheep. Unknown to him, God was using those years as part of a tailor-made program to prepare Moses for shepherding a much larger flock—the emerging nation of Israel. Only when Moses was truly ready did God appear to him in the burning bush and send him back to Egypt.

God's patience-building process may seem agonizingly slow to you, but remember, your response to God's "tutoring" is all-important. How fast are you learning the lessons you need to master in order to be ready for greater service when He calls? Right now, complete this prayer. "Dear LORD, because I know You want to use me in a significant way, please help me to learn the lesson in patience You have set before me today as I _____."

🔍 Insight: A Deadly Law for Men Only

Pharaoh's plot to kill all newborn Hebrew males not only would have curtailed the rapid growth of the Israelites, but would later have encouraged intermarriage between Hebrew women and Egyptian men, causing the people of Israel to lose their national identity.

EXODUS 3-6
MOSES' CALL & CREDENTIALS

♡ **Heart of The Passage:** Exodus 3; 5:1-6:13

It is God's resounding "I AM" that drowns out our weak "I can't."

📖 **Overview**

With his long period of desert exile drawing to a close, Moses becomes God's choice to lead the people out of bondage. When confronted by God in the burning bush, Moses is far from convinced he is the right man for the job! But once his objections have been answered, Moses goes forth to confront Pharaoh, armed with supernatural signs. True to God's prediction, Pharaoh not only refuses to let the people go, but increases their labors as well. As the people react with anger, God responds with assurance that His nation will indeed be redeemed.

Chapter 3:1-8	Chapter 3:9-22	Chapter 4	Chapter 5	Chapter 6
Moses' Call	Moses' Commission	Moses' Companion	Moses' Confrontation with Pharaoh	Moses' Confrontation with God
God's Man for Deliverance			God's Plan for Deliverance	

🚶 **Your Daily Walk**

Put yourself in Moses' sandals. You have been sent by God to deliver a people who have groaned under the burden of slavery for centuries. Upon your arrival, you encounter their oppressor, Pharaoh, and deliver the message God gave you. But instead of making things better, you only make them worse! You watch helplessly as Pharaoh increases the burden on your countrymen. What is your response?

Probably you'd do the same as Moses: Cry out to God in frustration. Perhaps you have been in Moses' sandals before if you have experienced the failure of a project you attempted for God. If so, God's fresh revelation of Himself—who He is, what He has done in the past, and what He promises to do in the future—should be as much of an encouragement to you as it was to Moses! God's promises are grounded in God's character. That's all Moses needed to know.

The same never-changing God who sustained a discouraged shepherd can do the same for you in difficult times. Find a hymnbook and browse through some of the faith-building refrains composed by those who learned firsthand that God is faithful. Their God is your God—and aren't you glad!

🔍 **Insight:** Take Away the Stubble, and You've Got Trouble

Bricks made with straw are stronger than those lacking it, because chemicals released by the decomposing straw make the clay more pliable and homogeneous. Archaeologists report that numerous structures built in biblical times with sun-dried bricks are still standing today.

EXODUS 7-10
FIRST NINE PLAGUES

 Heart of The Passage: Exodus 7

Those who say "No!" to God shouldn't be surprised when the locusts come calling.

Overview

When a person will not obey God willingly, God will often bring to bear circumstances that force him to obey God unwillingly. Such is the case with the reluctant Pharaoh of Egypt. God sends a series of nine national calamities involving insects, disease, and nature, in order to impress upon Pharaoh the importance of obedience. In half-hearted rebellion, Pharaoh repeatedly refuses to honor his promises and release the people. The stage is set for the tenth and climactic plague.

Ch. 7	Ch. 8:1-15	Ch. 8:16-19	Ch. 8:20-32	Ch. 9:1-7	Ch. 9:8-12	Ch. 9:13-35	Ch. 10:1-20	Ch. 10:21-29
Blood	Frogs	Lice	Flies	Livestock	Boils	Hail	Locusts	Darkness

THE GODS OF EGYPT VS. THE GOD OF ISRAEL (SEE 12:12)

 Your Daily Walk

Darkness and hail. Locusts and flies. Frogs and blood. What possible connection could there be between the 10 plagues? Did God have a reason for selecting those particular calamities? Why didn't He use high taxes, air pollution, inflation, "chariot recalls"? You know, the kinds of things we wrestle with today?

The key is found in 12:12: "Against all the gods of Egypt I will execute judgment." Every one of the 10 plagues represented an attack on an object of worship in Egypt: the Nile River, the sun god Re, the frog-goddess Haqt, the fly-god Uatchit, the protector-god Seth (who supposedly kept away locusts), the Pharaoh himself. The Egyptians had forsaken the Creator and in His place substituted the creation. So God used 10 "visual aids" to turn their eyes (and their worship) back to Him.

And that raises a penetrating question: If God were to bring 10 plagues upon your nation today—10 attacks upon objects of worship in your land—what might He use? Is there any evidence that He is doing precisely that? If so, what should your response be in the light of Pharaoh's sad experience?

 **Insight:** If You Thought Yesterday's Plague Was Bad...

Each succeeding plague was more intense and severe than its predecessor. The first four plagues produced only discomfort for the people. The fifth brought death to the cattle; the sixth produced physical pain; the seventh and eighth brought economic chaos; the ninth induced mental and emotional panic; and the tenth brought death to every Egyptian household.

EXODUS 11-12
TENTH PLAGUE, PASSOVER, & EXODUS

♡ **Heart of The Passage:** Exodus 12:1-28

The blood of Christ is the seal of the testament.

📖 **Overview**

Nine devastating plagues, and still Pharaoh will not budge! But the tenth and last plague—the slaying of the firstborn (of both man and animal) in every Egyptian household—brings about the long-awaited deliverance of Israel. To escape the terrible judgment on the firstborn, each Israelite household observes the Passover by substituting the death of a lamb for the death of a child. With no further resistance from Pharaoh, all Israel begins its exodus from Egypt.

CHAPTER 11	CHAPTER 12:1-28	CHAPTER 12:29-36	CHAPTER 12:37-51
Final Plague	First Passover	Firstborn Destroyed	Final Goodbye
"GO, SERVE THE LORD, AS YOU HAVE SAID" (12:31)			

🔍 **Insight:** Christ, Our Passover Lamb

Notice how the details of the Passover parallel the events surrounding the death of Christ.

Passover	_Christ_
The sacrifice must be a lamb (12:3).	Christ was the lamb of God (I Corinthians 5:7).
The lamb must be without spot or blemish (12:5).	Christ was without spot or blemish (I Peter 1:18-19).
The lamb must be in the prime of life when offered (12:5).	Christ was in the prime of His manhood when He died (John 8:57).
Lamb's blood was shed that Israel might have life (12:23).	Christ's blood was shed that the world might have life (John 3:16).

 Your Daily Walk

Death is never pleasant. Multiple deaths are considered disasters. So imagine the national impact when at least one member of each family in Egypt died overnight. But it was all necessary to prove to a stubborn Pharaoh that there is one true God. Deliverance for the Israelites came through faith in the blood applied to their doorposts.

Centuries later, Jesus Christ, the Lamb of God, gave His life to free men from bondage to sin. The question remains: Has His blood been applied to the doorposts of your heart? If so, thank Him again for the suffering He endured for you. If not, what better time than right now to pray: "Jesus, thank You for Your death on the cross. I receive You as my Redeemer from sin and as my Passover Lamb."

EXODUS 13-15
CROSSING THE RED SEA

♡ Heart of The Passage: Exodus 13:17-14:31

I need never distrust my God for cloth or bread while the lilies flourish and the ravens are fed.

📖 Overview

Delivering the people from Egyptian bondage is only the first step in God's plan to bring the Israelites to the Promised Land of Canaan. Many obstacles lie ahead. Pharaoh, whose heart is again hardened, sends his armies in pursuit of Moses and the people. Trapped between the Red Sea and the rapidly approaching chariots of Egypt, the people cry out in desperation, and God answers in a miraculous fashion. The Red Sea parts, the nation crosses over on dry ground, and shouts of panic turn to hymns of praise as the Egyptian army disappears in a watery grave.

Chapter 13	Chapter 14	Chapter 15
Provision	Protection	Praise
A Pillar of Cloud and Fire	A Path Through the Red Sea	A Psalm of Moses

🚶 Your Daily Walk

Little children don't always know what's best for them. If you don't believe that, just turn a child loose in an unfenced yard near a busy intersection, or leave your medicine cabinet unlocked. No, children don't have the wisdom of adults. That's why God provides parents—to help children survive to adulthood.

When the Israelites left Egypt, they were like a large band of children, not knowing what was best for them. But, like a loving father, God provided guidance, protection, food, water, and instruction to teach them how to enjoy a "grown-up" relationship with Him. Patiently and thoroughly He showed them what it meant to rely on Him in every facet of life, to depend upon His daily provision.

Has God placed you in a wilderness situation? Remember, you are there to learn a lesson in trusting God. Attach a safety pin to your lapel or collar today as a reminder of your dependence upon the Father. (It might even give you a conversation starter.)

🔍 Insight: What Color Is the Red Sea?

The Red Sea is a narrow body of water that stretches in a southeasterly direction from Suez to the Gulf of Arden for about 1,300 miles. Surprisingly enough, the Red Sea is usually bright turquoise in color. However, algae grow periodically in the water. When they die, the sea becomes reddish-brown, thus giving it the name Red Sea.

EXODUS 16-18
JOURNEY TO SINAI

♡ **Heart of The Passage:** Exodus 16:1-17:7

Complaining is the art of collecting petty annoyances.

📖 **Overview**

When Israel left Egypt, there were two things the people could do well: make bricks and complain. They now develop the latter ability to a fine art. As supplies decrease, complaints increase. When their resources run out, God supplies manna, quail, and water in abundance to demonstrate that He is now their reliable source of supply. Israel fights (and wins) its first military battle. And Moses, following the advice of his father-in-law, delegates some of his responsibilities to 70 capable assistants.

Chapter 16	Chapter 17:1-7	Chapter 17:8-16	Chapter 18
Hunger in the Wilderness	Thirst in Rephidim	Victory Over Amalek	Victory Over Exhaustion
Grumbling		Fighting	Delegating

🚶 **Your Daily Walk**

Start with a basic, two-door car loaded with luggage. Add a father, mother, and three children under the age of 10. Aim the car at a destination 500 miles down the road (such as Grandma's house). After 350 miles have passed, examine the scene. What shape is the "traveling circus" in now?

Magnify that basic situation 600,000 times over, move it back some 3,500 years, and you begin to understand Moses' predicament in Exodus 16. The thrill of freedom and the excitement of the exodus were soon erased by the discomforts of travel. Gratitude gave way to grumbling during the long desert trek.

Are you inclined to complain when things don't go as you think they should? Moses' words to Israel are timeless: "Your complaints are not against us, but against the Lord" (16:8).

On the other hand, one of the best indicators of your love for God is a contented spirit that expresses itself in thanksgiving. Get out your best card stock and write a thank-you note to God for some of the blessings you may have been taking for granted: health, peace, family, friends, employment, personal freedoms. Then mail it to yourself. In a day or two, you'll be twice blessed to read it again!

🔍 **Insight:** What's on the Menu?

Though God faithfully provided manna for 40 years, it should not be assumed that manna was the sum total of Israel's diet. They took numerous herds and flocks out of Egypt (12:38; 17:3) and were able to buy other food and water along the way (Deuteronomy 2:6-7).

EXODUS 19-20
THE TEN COMMANDMENTS

 Heart of The Passage: Exodus 20:1-17

If God had wanted a permissive society, He would have given us the Ten Suggestions.

 Overview

For the first time in four centuries, the Israelites are free to worship and walk with their holy God. But how do they approach God? What are His righteous demands? At Mount Sinai, Moses prepares the people to receive the Commandments, a body of law which they promise to obey—even before it is delivered! After two days of purification, the nation witnesses an awesome display of God's majesty as He descends in a thick cloud to deliver the Ten Commandments, the broad moral principles which will guide the new nation and set it apart from its pagan neighbors.

Chapter 19:1-15	Chapter 19:16-25	Chapter 20:1-17	Chapter 20:18-26
Cleansing the People	Cautioning the People	Commanding the People	Comforting the People
Thunder and Clouds		Ten Commandments	

 Your Daily Walk

What is missing in the following story? A brain surgeon is at home planting a garden when he receives word that an emergency case needs his immediate attention. He jumps in his car, drives to the hospital, strides into the operating room, and immediately begins to operate on the dying man.

Two items are clearly missing: (1) the all-important step of scrubbing up before the surgery, and (2) the name of a good lawyer to handle the almost certain malpractice suit!

Just as a doctor must scrub up before surgery, so must the Christian "scrub up" before entering the presence of a holy God in worship and prayer. The Israelites participated in symbolic acts of cleansing (19:10) in preparation for God's descent on Mount Sinai. The same God who desired purity from the Israelites requires pure hearts from those who approach Him today (Psalm 66:18; 1 John 1:9).

Is unconfessed sin soiling your relationship with God and keeping you from fellowship with Him? Talk to Him about that now. Then put a bar of soap by your Bible to remind you of the importance of scrubbing up regularly in your walk with God.

 Insight: When It Comes to God's Law, Take It Personal!

Though the Law was designed to govern the conduct of a nation, Exodus 20 uses the singular *you*, showing that the character of a nation depends upon the proper conduct of its citizens.

DAILY DEVOTIONS

EXODUS 21-24
CIVIL & CEREMONIAL LAWS

♡ **Heart of The Passage:** Exodus 24

Expedients are for the hour; principles are for the ages.

📖 **Overview**

At Mount Sinai, God delivers to Israel's leader not just the Ten Commandments, but also an extensive body of civil and ceremonial laws designed to regulate all aspects of Israel's life. The section you will read today contains the civil and social regulations which comprise "the Book of the Covenant" (24:7). Levites and priests, offerings and feasts, services and sacrifices—all are dealt with in meticulous detail. After receiving assurances from the people, "All that the LORD has said will we do" (24:7), Moses returns to the mountain, where for 40 more days he receives additional instructions from the Lord.

Chapter 21	Chapter 22	Chapter 23	Chapter 24
Law of Relationships	Law of Restitution	Law of Priests and Feasts	Law on Tablets of Stone
Civil		Ceremonial	Certain

🚶 **Your Daily Walk**

What does the Bible have to say about television? How about Sunday football? Where would you turn in your Bible to find day-care centers discussed? Or movies? Or smoking? What about birth control? Or rock music? Or recreational vehicles? Or horoscopes? Or the Internet?

If you go to your Bible expecting a detailed answer for every situation you encounter today, you will come away disappointed and discouraged. Even the seemingly exhaustive regulations of chapters 20-23 leave as much unsaid as they do said! But where God has seen fit not to provide particulars (either in Moses' day or in yours), He has supplied principles which help you to determine His mind in every situation. His Word, though ancient, is always relevant.

Prove it to yourself. Start with the list of 21st-century activities given above in the opening paragraph of "Your Daily Walk" (and add it to other activities you may be wrestling with). Can you suggest a principle from your reading of chapters 20-23 that will help you determine your level of participation in each of those activities?

🔍 **Insight:** The Mosaic Law, Expanded Version

In Exodus 20:1-17, God gives the law in summary fashion, and in 20:22-23:19, He provides a detailed amplification. In the first section God lays down broad moral principles; in the second, He gives specific applications of those principles to everyday life.

PLAN FOR THE TABERNACLE

♡ Heart of The Passage: Exodus 26

Life ought not merely to contain acts of worship; it should be an act of worship.

📖 Overview

What exactly was it that took Moses 40 days to write down while on Mount Sinai? As you read today's section (and the chapters that follow), you will discover the answer. Moses is receiving from God the detailed blueprint for the "church in the wilderness," which would be the tabernacle, Israel's place of worship. In minute detail Moses learns about the furnishings, coverings, curtains, and courtyard. Everything is to be built "according to its pattern which you were shown on the mountain" (26:30). The description moves from the inside out, reflecting not the perspective of man looking in, but of God looking out. True religion originates with a holy God.

CHAPTER 25	CHAPTER 26	CHAPTER 27
Furnishings	Coverings	Courtyard
PATTERN OF WORSHIP	PLACE OF WORSHIP	

🚶 Your Daily Walk

Put down this study guide. Close your eyes. Visualize the living room in your house, and make a mental list of every piece of furniture and decorative item in it. Now can you do the same with the furniture in the tabernacle? (Hint: There are four pieces inside and two outside.) Can you recall the function of each? More important, can you identify one picture which each piece suggests regarding the person and work of Jesus Christ, who came to "tabernacle" with men and women forever? (If you have time, reading Hebrews 8-10 will make the tabernacle unforgettable!)

🔍 Insight: Arrangement of the Tabernacle

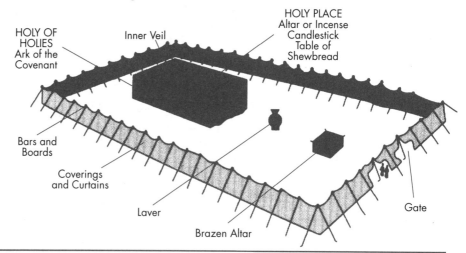

EXODUS 28-31
BLUEPRINT FOR THE PRIESTS

♡ **Heart of The Passage:** Exodus 28

Does God seem far away? Guess who moved.

📖 **Overview**

After describing the place of worship (the tabernacle), Moses goes on to detail the people of worship (the priests, Israel's representatives before God). Everything about them is special, from the clothing they wear to the elaborate rituals they perform in leading the worship of the nation. Both they and the implements of worship they use require special purification, as befitting those in the service of a holy God. Even the builders who are selected to follow the divine blueprint for the tabernacle are handpicked by God for their skill and Spirit-filled craftsmanship.

CHAPTER 28	CHAPTER 29	CHAPTER 30	CHAPTER 31
Priestly Clothing	Priestly Consecration	Priestly Conduct	Tabernacle Craftsmen
PREPARATION FOR THE MINISTER		PREPARATION FOR THE MINISTRY	

 Your Daily Walk

Apart from the symbolism found in the tabernacle, its foremost significance was this: The tabernacle represented God come to dwell among men and women, the beacon of God's presence among His people. In addition, the priest's role was to act as a go-between, a bridge-builder, someone who could stand on behalf of sinful humanity before a holy God.

In the New Testament there is a beautiful blending of these two themes. Where does God dwell today? He continues to dwell among people. How has He seen fit to do this? By indwelling those who have turned their lives over to Him (1 Corinthians 6:19). And whom has He called to be priests today, bringing sinful people back to their holy God? The very ones He indwells (1 Peter 2:9)! You are both the tabernacle God indwells, and the priest God empowers to call men and women back to Himself.

If God were to give you the privilege of building a "gospel bridge" into someone's life today, would you be ready? willing? able? Tell Him so, right now!

🔍 **Insight:** And Don't Forget the Sabbath Day

The commandment concerning the Sabbath had already been given in the Law. It is interesting that this fourth commandment is mentioned again in conjunction with instructions for the workmen (31:12-17). God had commissioned the people to a work especially sacred; He had provided for carrying out the work by especially equipped men. How easy it would have been for them to imagine that in doing this work they might dispense with the Sabbath observance. God's work must be done in His way.

EXODUS 32-34
ISRAEL'S IDOLATRY & MOSES' INTERCESSION

 Heart of The Passage: Exodus 32

If your face reflected your God, what would you see when you looked in the mirror?

Overview

While Moses receives God's laws on the mountain, the Israelites are busy on the plains below. Concluding that their leader has died in the presence of God, they fashion their gold jewelry into a replica of an Egyptian god and turn the camp into a grotesque pagan party. Moses returns and in righteous anger shatters the two stone tablets, destroys the golden calf, and orders the Levites to purge the camp of the guilty Israelites. But though the newly adopted covenant between God and His people has been shattered (as illustrated in the two broken tablets), repentance and restoration are only a prayer away.

Chapter 32	Chapter 33	Chapter 34
Worshiping the Golden Calf	Moving the Tabernacle	Renewing the Ten Commandments
Idolatry and Intercession		Recommitment and Renewal

 Your Daily Walk

Could it be the golden calf episode (Chapter 32) is also a 15th-century B.C. parable of a 21st-century A.D. phenomenon?

With assurances of the nation's obedience and love (24:7), Moses left to be with God on the mountain. No sooner was he gone than false worship and gross wickedness replaced the flimsy promises which the people had made. Though their lips vowed allegiance, their hearts were far from God. And as soon as their leader departed, the people's true character emerged.

In the same way, the church's Leader has gone to be with God for a time, leaving His church behind to carry out His commands. But worldliness and sin, idolatry and preoccupation, have dimmed His final words to "go... preach the gospel to every creature" (Mark 16:15). Idolatry couldn't happen in your life, in your family, in your church, could it? What should you do if it has (1 Corinthians 10:11-14)?

Insight: Reflecting God to the Nation (34:29-35)

Moses remained on Mount Sinai 40 days longer (34:28), receiving additional instructions from the LORD, and again God carved the Ten Commandments onto tablets of stone. When Moses returned to the camp, it was impossible for him to conceal the fact that he had been in the presence of the LORD. His face made that clear to all those around him! Today your task is the same: to reflect the glory of Jesus Christ to others around you. How are you doing with your assignment?

EXODUS 35-40

TABERNACLE ERECTED & OCCUPIED BY GOD

♡ Heart of The Passage: Exodus 36, 40

Revival is nothing more, or less, than a fresh commitment to obey God.

📖 Overview

The book of Exodus closes with the record of how the tabernacle and priestly garments are completed exactly as God instructed. The people donate the materials, and the chosen artisans do the work. Moses inspects the finished product, the furnishings are set in place, and Aaron and his sons are anointed for service. Finally, God declares His satisfaction by filling the tent with His glory. For the next 480 years, the tabernacle will remain the focal point of the nation's worship.

Chapter 35	Chapters 36-38	Chapter 39	Chapter 40:1-33	Chapter 40:34-38
Contributions by the People	Construction by the Craftsmen	Consecration by Moses	Finishing the Tabernacle	Filling the Tabernacle
TABERNACLE ORGANIZED			TABERNACLE OCCUPIED	

🚶 Your Daily Walk

Today you will complete an important part of your journey through the Pentateuch. But today's reading will require extra discipline! You have already read much of this material before in chapters 25-28. There Moses set forth the plan for constructing and erecting the tabernacle. Now in chapters 36-39 you'll study the performance of that plan as Moses' instructions are carried out to the letter, making the tabernacle a reality.

But don't miss the point. The requirement was 100 percent compliance. It's like baking a cake. Follow the recipe to the letter and you get a delicious dessert; omit some ingredients or instructions and you get a culinary catastrophe. When it comes to holiness or obedience, halfway measures will not do. You are not to love the LORD with most of your heart, a portion of your soul, and a tithe of your mind.

As you carefully read through these last chapters of Exodus, ask God to reveal any areas in your life where you have become halfhearted or sloppy. The ongoing construction of your life as God's temple demands no less care than the building of Israel's tabernacle if your life is to radiate His glory and bear witness of His name to the community around you.

🔍 Insight: What Do You Do with Too Much Gold?

In view of the fact that the weight of the precious metals used in building the tabernacle ran into the tons (38:24-29), it is an even greater marvel that the budget for this building project was exceeded by the donations (36:3-7).

OFFERINGS OF PRAISE

 Heart of The Passage: Leviticus 1

God knew all about the wickedness of the world, and still thought it worth saving.

Overview

With the tabernacle completed, God now gives Moses instructions regarding the five types of sacrifices that would be offered in the tabernacle. Three of them—the sweet savor offerings—were voluntary expressions of worship tailored to the person's ability to give. Two nonsweet savor offerings were required when sin had broken fellowship with God. In the burnt offering, the worshiper declared his total commitment to God. Through the meal offering he acknowledged that his material possessions belonged wholly to the LORD. By means of the peace offering, the worshiper publicly expressed his thanks or made a vow of spiritual service to God.

CHAPTER 1	CHAPTER 2	CHAPTER 3
Burnt Offering	Meal Offering	Peace Offering

SACRIFICES FOR THOSE IN FELLOWSHIP WITH GOD

Q Insight: Sacrifices for the 21ˢᵗ Century

Animal sacrifices, so essential to Old Testament worship, ceased with Christ's once-for-all-time sacrifice on the cross. Yet Peter tells us that all believers are priests who should continually offer up spiritual sacrifices acceptable to God (1 Peter 2:5).

 Your Daily Walk

Today you will read about three Old Testament sacrifices prescribed for each Israelite. But did you know that the New Testament describes at least three "sacrifices" prescribed for each believer—three ways for you to offer a sacrifice to God today?

Instead of a whole burnt offering, you can offer your body as "a living sacrifice . . . to God" (Romans 12:1). In place of a meal offering, you might offer from your material possessions "an acceptable sacrifice" by helping someone in financial need (like the Philippians did for Paul; see Philippians 4:18). Instead of the peace offering, you could offer the "sacrifice of praise" to God (Hebrews 13:15), a verbal expression of thanksgiving for His care and provision in your life.

Today would be a good time to offer a sweet savor sacrifice to God. Take one of the three sacrifices described above and put it to work by committing each part of your body to God's service (living sacrifice), sharing publicly God's goodness in your life (sacrifice of praise), or writing a check to someone in need (acceptable sacrifice).

LEVITICUS 4-7
OFFERINGS FOR RESTORATION

 Heart of The Passage: Leviticus 4-5

Life is a long lesson in humility.

 **Overview**

In addition to the three sweet savor offerings, God gives the Israelites two non-sweet savor sacrifices. Both are required when sin has broken fellowship with God. The sin offering, covering sins of uncleanness, neglect, or thoughtlessness, provided restoration for the sinner while teaching the seriousness of sin and its consequences. The trespass offering, covering sins of injury to God and to others, provided not only for the restoration of the sinner, but for compensation to the injured party as well.

Chapter 4	Chapter 5	Chapters 6-7
Sin Offering	Trespass Offering	A Second Look at Offerings
Sacrifices to Restore Fellowship		Sacrifices Reviewed

 Your Daily Walk

In the margin, list five unpleasant but beneficial experiences from daily life. List things you dislike doing, but know they are good for you. (Hint: You might want to start in the dentist's office.)

If you're normal, you probably don't enjoy the whine of the dentist's drill; but after all the poking and drilling and bitter taste, you find you feel a lot better. Being corrected by a boss when you've made a mistake isn't pleasant either, but afterwards you're glad your boss cared enough to confront you with the truth.

In the Christian life there are some equally painful but profitable exercises—like obeying the biblical principle of restitution. When an Israelite caused injury to another, God's command was clear: "Make it up to him." You, as a Christian, likewise have an obligation to repay those whom you have injured.

Think back over the past week. Is there someone whose character or possessions you have damaged? Have you asked for forgiveness? (That's hard!) Have you repaid what you owe? (That's harder still!) Take the initiative today to offer a trespass offering to God. You'll find the peace of mind and restored relationship well worth the pain.

Insight: And If You Need a Model to Follow . . .

Zacchaeus, the tax collector who trusted Christ (Luke 19:1-10), beautifully illustrates restitution at work. The law told a sinner to restore what he had taken or damaged, plus 20 percent. Zacchaeus in his gratitude offered to restore what he had taken fourfold!

HOLY OFFICE OF THE PRIEST

 Heart of The Passage: Leviticus 9:23-10:7

No one can build a reputation on what he's going to do tomorrow.

 **Overview**

Israel's tabernacle, the place of communion with God through sacrifice, is entrusted to the custody of Aaron and his sons. The priestly corps must undergo a 10-step consecration process and a seven-day dedication period before they can begin their ministry of mediation. God's blessing—made visible by His fiery presence—suddenly turns into a curse as judgment falls on two of Aaron's disobedient sons. Their deaths remind all Israel of the solemn responsibility of serving a holy God. Obedience, not expedience, should mark the people of God.

Chapter 8	Chapter 9	Chapter 10
Consecration of the Priestly Ministry	Inauguration of the Priestly Ministry	Regulation of the Priestly Ministry
Dedication	Duty	

 Your Daily Walk

Nothing is as hard to gain, and as easy to lose, as a good reputation. One philosopher has observed, "To have lost your reputation is to be dead among the living." Perhaps as a child you heard your parents say, "Remember now, what you do and say reflects on us." Your parents were telling you that the family's reputation was either being tarnished or enhanced by your actions.

Perhaps that is why God responded with such frightening judgment upon Nadab and Abihu. By their carelessness and disobedience, they threatened God's very reputation both inside and outside the nation of Israel—a grave sin indeed.

Your life as a Christian is the only "Bible" some people will ever read. Do you reveal to others a holy God by your commitment to holiness, or do you smear the reputation of God with an inconsistent life? Write out this thought on an index card and carry it with you today:

"God's reputation is at stake in my life. I want to maintain it, not stain it."

Then each time you are tempted to stray from God's holiness, pull out that card. Read it; think about it; then let God strengthen you to be wholly—and holy—His!

Q Insight: The Danger of Failing to Live Up to Your Name

Nadab ("noble, virtuous") and Abihu ("God is my father") were in danger of damaging more than the reputation of their God. If allowed to continue in their sinful ways, they would have besmirched both their families and the godly names they carried.

LEVITICUS 11-15
HOLINESS IN DAILY LIFE

 **Heart of The Passage:** Leviticus 11:44-47; 13:59; 14:54-57

The LORD has two heavens to dwell in, and the holy heart is one of them.

Overview

Worshiping a holy God demands a holy people. For this reason God gives Israel a series of regulations dealing with ceremonial uncleanness. Four areas are specified: dietary laws (describing edible and non-edible animals); childbirth matters; leprosy and other skin disorders; and bodily discharges. Each set of commands follows a general pattern. The worshiper's defilement is first described, then the means for regaining his purity are prescribed. It's a lengthy, detailed section because holiness demands attention to detail.

CHAPTER 11	CHAPTER 12	CHAPTERS 13-14	CHAPTER 15
Purity in Diet	Purity in Delivery	Purity in Disease	Purity in Discharges
AVOIDABLE DEFILEMENT	UNAVOIDABLE DEFILEMENT		

 ## Your Daily Walk

When you read the command in Leviticus 11:44, "Be holy; for I am holy," what do you think?

Isn't God demanding something impossible and unattainable from His people? Isn't He being unreasonable when He says, "Be holy"? Why, from a human point of view, the task seems impossible.

That is precisely the point! It is impossible by human efforts alone to live up to the righteous demands of a holy God. But rather than frustrate you, God wants to teach you. The law was designed to teach the Israelites to be dependent upon God. Just as He provided sacrifices and rituals for cleansing His less-than-perfect people, so He wants to teach you that only through the supernatural provision of a sinless Savior, Jesus Christ, can you hope to achieve holiness.

Paul puts it this way: "As you have therefore received Christ Jesus the LORD [by faith, trusting in Him], so walk in Him [by faith, trusting in Him]" (Colossians 2:6). In Christ's strength you can live a holy and pure life. Complete this thought from Leviticus 11:44: "You shall be holy [how? when? where? with whom?]; for I am holy." Then work today on developing the habit of holiness in one area of your life.

Insight: Leprosy Then and Now

It is doubtful that modern-day leprosy (which cripples and disfigures) is the same as Levitical or New Testament "leprosy" (which was a white scaly disease, much like eczema or psoriasis).

LEVITICUS 16-17
HOLINESS IN NATIONAL LIFE

 Heart of The Passage: Leviticus 16

Jesus Christ is God's perfect provision for imperfect people.

 Overview

The great Day of Atonement observed each year was Israel's most significant act of worship. On that day, the nation gathered to watch in expectation as the high priest entered the Holy of Holies with the blood atonement which would cover the sins of the entire nation for another year. Because blood was the central ingredient in Israel's national and personal forgiveness, God prohibited the use of blood for any purpose other than sacrifice to Him.

Chapter 16	Chapter 17
Day of Atonement	Defilement by Blood
Holiness of the Nation	

 Your Daily Walk

What would you do if God gave you the responsibility of atoning for your own sins? What would you offer as payment to satisfy His righteous demands: the deed to your house? your savings account? your awards and achievements? your spotless reputation? As sincere as these offerings might be, they would never be adequate to make amends for your sins.

Each year, as the nation of Israel stood in front of the tabernacle on the Day of Atonement and watched the high priest carry the blood of the sin offering into the Holy of Holies, the people were reminded again that atonement was God's idea. It was His provision for forgiveness of sinful men. He took the initiative to establish a sacrifice of atonement which provided a blood substitute for the guilty nation.

Just as God provided the way to cover Israel's sins, so too He has sent His own Son as the once-for-all-time atonement for your sins (1 John 2:2). As you rejoice over that wonderful truth, make a list of three friends who need to experience Christ's forgiveness of sins. Pray today for each of the three names, and be ready to share a word of testimony when God opens the door.

Q Insight: No Private Sacrifices Allowed!

The restrictions against private sacrifices outside the tabernacle (17:3-4) were to prevent the people from copying their pagan neighbors, who often poured their blood sacrifices into the ground as food for their gods. Only properly ordained priests in the proper location (the tabernacle) could offer Israel's sacrifices.

LEVITICUS 18-20
HOLINESS FOR THE INDIVIDUAL

♡ Heart of The Passage: Leviticus 19

The primary test of life is not service but love for both man and God.

📖 Overview

In addition to the regulations governing national holiness, God provides Israel with laws governing personal conduct and purity in relation to the family, the community, and society in general. Because obedience is His primary concern, God requires that violators of His laws be punished, and that the punishment be appropriate to the crime committed. God's strict guidelines for living reflect His desire that His people "be holy . . . for I the Lord am holy, and have separated you from the peoples, that you should be mine" (20:26).

Chapter 18	Chapter 19	Chapter 20
Purity in Morals	Practice of Love	Penalty for Disobedience

HOLINESS FOR THE INDIVIDUAL

🚶 Your Daily Walk

"You shall love your neighbor as yourself" (19:18) rolls off the tongue with a familiar ease. But putting it into practice is another matter. Of all God's commands, it may be one of the most difficult to keep. The reason? Because loving your neighbor means you must be involved in the life of your neighbor. That's hard to do because a human being's natural tendency is toward selfishness, not selflessness.

The Old Testament law was a challenge to keep because it made very specific demands on the individual. If an Israelite had questions about how to relate to his neighbor, the law provided the answers (19:9-18). The New Testament is just as demanding—especially when it speaks of your relationship to your "neighbor." Jesus' story of the Good Samaritan (Luke 10:25-37) makes it clear that your "neighbor" is anyone near you who needs your help and whose need God has equipped you to meet.

Even if you live alone, there are people around you who need your loving involvement. Put God's command to love your neighbor into practice today by seeking out someone who needs help with yardwork, housework, or homework. Assist them in love, and treat them as you would yourself!

🔍 Insight: "Do Like Me to Be Like Me"

Nearly 30 times in chapters 18-22 we read God's words: "I am the Lord," and, "Be holy . . . for I the Lord your God am holy." Without a doubt, the holiness of the Redeemer is the all-compelling reason for His insistence on practices of purity by the redeemed.

HOLY PRIESTS & HOLY FEASTS

 Heart of The Passage: Leviticus 21

It is easier to follow the leader than to lead the followers.

 Overview

Privilege often carries with it responsibility, and in the case of Israel's priests, the responsibilities of serving a holy God become quite demanding. The priests must avoid defilement which others might ordinarily experience. They must be without physical defect in order to serve in the sanctuary. They must bear the responsibility for maintaining purity in Israel's sacrificial worship. They must preside at Israel's yearly feasts and sacred assemblies. It is indeed a demanding assignment to lead a nation in corporate worship of a holy God—a privilege not to be taken lightly or entered into casually.

Chapter 21:1-15	Chapter 21:15-24	Chapter 22	Chapter 23
Disqualification of a Priest Through Defilement	Disqualification of a Priest Through Defect	Duties of a Priest in Ceremonies	Duties of a Priest in Celebrations
Holy Priest			Holy Feasts

 Your Daily Walk

If you discovered that your dining room had been "bugged," would you have some embarrassing conversations to explain?

Unfortunately, in many Christian homes the main course for Sunday dinner is often "roast preacher." It's an easy habit to slip into, but one which can produce harm and bitterness.

In Israel's system of worship, the priests carried much of the responsibility for leading corporate worship. Today the church no longer has a "priestly class," but it does have those specially gifted, trained, and set apart for the work of the ministry (1 Timothy 3; Titus 1). Like the priests of Old Testament times, these leaders have given freely of their time and energy in order to lead you in worship.

How often do you "remember those who rule over you" (Hebrews 13:7)? Take a few minutes to write a thank-you note to your pastor or church leader, expressing gratitude for the consistent spiritual investment that person makes in your life.

 Insight: Probing a Priestly Prohibition

Priests with physical handicaps were excluded from offering sacrifices (21:17-21), though they were entitled to the privileges of priesthood such as eating the priestly portion (21:22). God was not relegating them to second-class status, but merely showing that the special service of sacrificing unblemished animals before a holy God required unblemished priests.

LEVITICUS 24-27
HOLINESS IN THE LAND

 **Heart of The Passage:** Leviticus 25

If you owned everything your heart desired, chances are your heart would desire something else.

 Overview

The closing chapters of Leviticus contain a variety of instructions for Israel when the people occupy the Promised Land. Oil and bread must be provided for the sanctuary. The death penalty must fall on those who blaspheme the name of God. The land must be given periodic rest during the Sabbatical and Jubilee years. God promises to honor obedience to His commands, and reward disobedience with stern judgment. The work of the LORD must be faithfully supported by the tithes of God's people, and vows must not be entered into lightly.

CHAPTER 24	CHAPTER 25	CHAPTER 26	CHAPTER 27
Provision for the Sanctuary	Protection for the Land	Obedience and Disobedience	Vows and Tithes
HONORING GOD'S PROPERTY		HONORING GOD'S PROGRAM	

Your Daily Walk

Ownership is always a sensitive issue. People are born with an innate desire to possess. Children at play argue loudly, "That's mine!" Though adults usually tend to be more civilized about it, you'll find the same sentiment voiced repeatedly: "I want what's mine!"

God recognized this tendency in His people and instituted the Year of Jubilee to help teach them a crucial spiritual truth. Every fiftieth year, all land that had been sold was to be returned to its original owner. And every acre of land was to remain uncultivated in order to remind the nation that the land belonged not to them, but to God. He would give it to them (25:2), and they would enjoy it, not as owners, but as aliens and tenants (25:23).

How do you view your possessions? Do you hold on to them tightly, or have you recognized them as something graciously "loaned" to you by God? Remember, a steward is someone who owns nothing, but is responsible for everything entrusted to his care. To reinforce that truth, take one room of your house and inventory everything in it. Then across the list, write these words: "Mine by stewardship, His by ownership!" Get the picture?

Insight: Captivity Foretold

One of the earliest predictions of the Assyrian and Babylonian captivities occurs in today's reading (26:33-35). Israel knew from the start what would happen if the people disobeyed God's Word. Yet, centuries later it would come true—to the letter.

NUMBERS 1-4
COUNTING THE PEOPLE

♡ Heart of The Passage: Numbers 1:1-3, 45-46

Your life can't go according to plan if you have no plan.

📖 Overview

The book of Numbers might well be called "the Census Book," for that is how it begins and ends. With the nation of Israel poised at Mount Sinai ready to begin its march to Canaan, God commands Moses to number the fighting men and Levites. A detailed blueprint is given for arranging the people both on the march and in the camp. In the intervening 430 years that the children of Israel lived in Egypt (Exodus 12:40), the nation's fighting force has grown to an impressive 603,550, suggesting a total population of several million.

Chapter 1	Chapter 2	Chapter 3	Chapter 4
Counting the Nation	Arranging the Camp	Arranging the Levites	Assigning the Levites
Numbering the People		Numbering the Priests	

🚶 Your Daily Walk

Censuses are prominent throughout the pages of Scripture. How many different censuses can you recall, excluding the two in Numbers? (If you think 0-1, numbers must leave you numb; 2-3, you can be counted on; 4 or more, you must work for the Census Bureau!)

Even more important than the presence of censuses in the Bible is the purpose behind them: to show that God is a God of order and detail. Confusion and disorder in your home, church, or private life are a sure sign that God-honoring principles are being overlooked (1 Corinthians 14:40). Pick an area of your Christian life where the goal of doing all things "decently and in order" has proven elusive. Write it in the margin, and make it the target of your prayer and planning this week. Remember, if you aim at nothing, you will hit it every time.

🔍 Insight: On Your Mark . . . Get Set . . . March!

Leviticus prepared the people for worship; Numbers prepares them for war. After reading today's section, summarize the census and the preparations for the march to Canaan.

Census of the warriors: _____ (total)

Census of the workers: _____ Levites (1 month upward)
                        _____ Levites (30-50 years)

Largest tribe: _____ Its population: _____

Smallest tribe: _____ Its population: _____

Who takes care of the tabernacle? _____

Who transports the tabernacle? _____

NUMBERS 5-8
CLEANSING THE PEOPLE

 **Heart of The Passage:** Numbers 6:1-7:11

The best exercise for strengthening the heart is reaching out and lifting people up.

Overview

Three weeks remain before the people leave Sinai to begin the last leg of their journey to Canaan. During this time Moses receives certain commands from God designed to cleanse the people and prepare them to enter the Promised Land. They must be free from immorality and jealousy; they must understand the binding nature of vows made to God; the Levites must realize the sacred nature of their calling. Through the generous gifts of the tribal leaders, the tabernacle implements and supplies are provided for the worship of the LORD.

Chapter 5	Chapter 6	Chapter 7	Chapter 8
Clean Morals	Commendable Vows	Consecrated Offerings	Clean Levites
Defilement	Dedication		

Your Daily Walk

What is the most important tool you will ever use in your service for God? (Write in the margin the first tool that comes to mind.)

Perhaps you thought of a book, or the Bible, or a God-given ability. Here's another tool you may not have considered: your body.

Any service you render for God in this life will be done through the use of your body. And while you may pride yourself on the way you discipline your mind, your body may be one of the most neglected tools God has entrusted to you.

The Old Testament man or woman who wanted to be used in God's service but was not eligible as a Levite or priest could take the Nazirite vow—a vow that involved abstaining from certain hindrances to holiness in order to be wholly devoted to the service of the LORD. It was a voluntary vow, difficult to get into and equally difficult to get out of. And yet it held the promise of personal blessing for those who successfully fulfilled it.

Is your body available to God today, cleansed and prepared for His use? Romans 12:1-2 will show you how, but only you can volunteer.

Insight: No Wine, Hair Cuts, or Corpses Allowed

The requirements of the Nazarite vow might seem strange unless understood in their symbolic sense. Wine symbolized comfort and enjoyment. Death represented defilement. Long hair stood for God-given strength and dignity. By avoiding the former and maintaining the latter, the Nazarite declared his total devotion to God.

NUMBERS 9-12
THE PEOPLE COMPLAINING

♡ **Heart of The Passage:** Numbers 10:11-13; 11:1-15

Some people ask the LORD to guide them; then they grab the steering wheel.

📖 **Overview**

The time has come for the final journey to Canaan. After a special celebration of the Passover, the people watch as the pillar of cloud begins to move. Trumpets blare forth the exciting news: It is time to march! But the thrill of expectation soon gives way to the tedium of travel, and Moses is faced with numerous problems: complaints about the travel conditions and the food, longings for the good old days in Egypt, greedy hoarding of the quail God supplies, and jealousy by Miriam and Aaron toward his position of leadership. In spite of the difficulties, the people finally arrive at Kadesh-barnea—on the doorstep of Canaan!

CHAPTER 9	CHAPTER 10	CHAPTER 11	CHAPTER 12
A Cloudy Pillar	A Call to March	A Complaining People	A Covetous Miriam
PREPARATIONS FOR THE JOURNEY		PROBLEMS ON THE JOURNEY	

 Your Daily Walk

How do you react when God's will for you turns out to be inconvenient? Do you think, *Maybe later, God, but not right now.*

For Israel, God's will was easily determined by the movement of the cloud covering the tabernacle. When it moved, they moved. When it lingered, they camped. At first glance that may seem like an exciting way to live—but consider the possibilities!

It is 3 a.m. You are sound asleep after a difficult 14-hour march, when the quiet desert air is shattered by the blast of a trumpet. Time to march! Or consider another scene. For three days now the cloud has hovered motionless. You sense that any minute it is going to move, so instead of unpacking that bulky tent and all those cooking pots, you just "live off the camel." Another day goes by. And another. Finally, you give in and begin the arduous task of unpacking. No sooner do you drive in the last tent peg when . . .

Obedience to God's will is not always convenient, but it is always profitable! Do you see a pillar of cloud moving in your life? What is it? And what do you suppose you ought to do about it?

🔍 **Insight:** Quail Dinner—All You Can Eat!

When God sent quail in response to the people's complaining, the least amount gathered by one person was 10 homers. One homer is 11 bushels. One bushel is 8 gallons. That makes a total of 880 gallons!

NUMBERS 13-16
SPYING OUT THE LAND

♡ **Heart of The Passage:** Numbers 13:1-2, 26-33; 14:20-35

So often the first screw that works loose in a person's head is the one that holds the tongue in place.

📖 **Overview**

Following the LORD's instructions, Moses selects one representative from each of the 12 tribes to form a scouting party. Their assignment: to spy out the defenses of the land and bring back a sample of the produce grown there. The 12 obey and, like many a committee, return with a divided report. Ten see only the obstacles; two see the opportunities. The nation, disheartened and faithless, threatens to stone Moses and return to Egypt rather than face what lies ahead. As a result, God condemns that unbelieving generation to 40 years of fruitless wandering in the wilderness.

CHAPTER 13	CHAPTER 14	CHAPTER 15	CHAPTER 16
A Divided Report	A Deadly Result	A Divine Code of Law	A Premature Death for Korah
TWELVE SPIES	WANDERING	REGULATIONS	

🔍 **Insight:** . . . 8 . . . 9 . . . 10 . . . You're Out! (14:22)

On 10 separate occasions the Israelites grumbled and murmured against God. Can you find what prompted each complaint?

Exodus 5:20-21 _____

Exodus 14:10-12 _____

Exodus 15:24 _____

Exodus 16:2-3 _____

Exodus 16:20, 27 _____

Exodus 17:2-3 _____

Exodus 32:1-4 _____

Numbers 11:1 _____

Numbers 11:4-5 _____

Numbers 13:26-14:3 _____

 Your Daily Walk

Every part of the human body gets tired eventually . . . except the tongue! It is no accident the Bible describes the tongue as sharp (Psalm 140:3), biting (Proverbs 25:23), and untamable (James 3:8).

Do you (like the Israelites) have trouble bringing your tongue under control? Then enlist the aid of your spouse or a close Christian friend in "Operation Salty Speech" (Colossians 4:6). Every time he or she catches you in an ungracious remark during the next seven days, you must pay 25 cents. Try it! What you lose in material wealth you'll more than regain in spiritual maturity.

NUMBERS 17-20
DYING IN THE WILDERNESS

♡ **Heart of The Passage:** Numbers 20:1-13

Sin produces a moment of gratification and an eternity of remorse.

📖 Overview

Throughout their wilderness wanderings, the children of Israel are reminded of two things: death and hope. Death as the result of their unbelief at Kadesh-barnea, and hope in the promise that God would still give His people a land of their own. God's authority continues to rest with Moses and Aaron, as demonstrated in the miracle of Aaron's budding rod. And the priests and Levites are still God's chosen servants to lead the nation in corporate worship. But death becomes the constant companion of the Israelites on their march: death in the sacrifices, death of the red cow for purification, and the death of the high priest Aaron.

Chapter 17	Chapter 18	Chapter 19	Chapter 20
Rod of Aaron	Responsibilities of the Levites	Red Cow	Rebellion of the People
Establishing the Priesthood		Enforcing National Purity	

🚶 Your Daily Walk

Find a hammer, nail, and piece of wood. Drive the nail halfway into the wood; then remove it carefully. What do you have left? (To make this a truly memorable experience, drive the nail into your front door, or substitute your favorite piece of furniture.)

That illustration from the world of carpentry provides a parable of the permanent results of sin. Once confessed, we receive God's full forgiveness (1 John 1:9)—like removing the nail from the piece of wood. But you may not be able to erase fully the scars which that sin has left behind.

Are you, like Moses, tempted to "strike a rock" when God has told you to "speak softly"? Weigh the consequences ahead of time. Christ not only died that sin might be forgiven; He died that sin might be avoided. Thank Him for a scar or nail hole you'll never have to carry because you were willing to say no to sin and yes to Him.

🔍 Insight: Cow in the Old, Savior in the New

Chapter 19 describes God's provision for the people's uncleanness by using water mingled with the ashes of a red cow. This curious rite becomes clearer in the light of Hebrews 9:11-14 as a foreshadowing of Jesus. Just as the ashes of the sin offering had a purifying effect when applied by water, so Jesus' offering for sin purifies everyone to whom it is applied by His Spirit.

DAILY DEVOTIONS

NUMBERS 21-25
THE BRASS SNAKE & BRASH SEER

 Heart of The Passage: Numbers 21-22

When opportunity knocks, a grumbler complains about the noise.

Overview

As the Israelites march to Canaan, they meet and defeat three enemies: the Canaanites, Amorites, and Bashanites. But on the heels of victory they suffer defeat at the hands of a peculiarly persistent foe: grumbling. Because of the people's constant complaining, God sends fiery snakes to chasten His rebellious nation. The threat of Israel's advance prompts the neighboring pagan nations to hire the prophet Balaam to bring down a curse upon God's people. But instead of a curse, Balaam delivers a sweeping witness to the glorious future of Yahweh's nation. What Balaam could not do with his voice, however, is accomplished by his evil influence, as the Israelites give in to idolatry and mixed marriage in defiance of God's law.

Chapter 21	Chapters 22-24	Chapter 25
Conquest and Complaint	Call and Prophecies of Balaam	Calamity in the Camp
Success	Sovereign Blessing	Sin

 Your Daily Walk

Find a small piece of sandpaper and tuck it in your pocket or purse. Then read the next few paragraphs thoughtfully and prayerfully.

In chapter 21 the nation Israel conquered three national powers. Smashing victories! Stunning triumphs! But for some of the people it wasn't enough. After all, they were still on the wrong side of the Jordan and didn't possess even a spadeful of the Promised Land. Their impatience led to criticism—and criticism to fiery judgment.

One key to consistency in the Christian life is simply giving God time to work. Rough edges take time to smooth. Growth to maturity never occurs overnight. But each day can be a step in the right direction.

Is God using a little sandpaper on your life right now? How can you cooperate with, rather than oppose, the work of the Master Carpenter?

Insight: Jesus and Numbers—They Go Together!

Look up the following verses to discover how each Old Testament passage provides a preview of Jesus Christ centuries before His birth:

Snake of brass (21:4-9; John 3:14)

Water from rocks (20:11; 1 Corinthians 10:4)

Manna (11:7-9; John 6:31-33)

NUMBERS 26-30
SECOND CENSUS

 Heart of The Passage: Numbers 26:52-56; 27:18-23

Every great person has first learned how, when, and whom to obey.

Overview

Now that the journey is virtually over, it is time for a second census—both to assess Israel's military strength and to apportion the soon-to-be conquered territory of Canaan. In addition, it is time to appoint Moses' successor—the one who will lead the people in their conquest. God's choice is Joshua, one of only two members of the generation that left Egypt to survive the wilderness wanderings and enter the Promised Land. Under Joshua's leadership, the nation will enjoy both military victory and spiritual vitality as they obey God's commands and fulfill their holy obligations.

Chapter 26	Chapter 27	Chapters 28-30
Another Numbering of the Nation	Another Leader for the Nation	Another Code of Worship for the Nation
Census	Succession	Ceremony

Insight: Tally Up the Second Census by Tribe (Fill In)

Tribe	1st Census	2nd Census	Tribe	1st Census	2nd Census
1. Reuben	46,500	_____	7. Ephraim	40,500	_____
2. Simeon	59,300	_____	8. Manasseh	32,200	_____
3. Gad	45,650	_____	9. Benjamin	35,400	_____
4. Judah	74,600	_____	10. Dan	62,700	_____
5. Issachar	54,400	_____	11. Asher	41,500	_____
6. Zebulun	57,400	_____	12. Naphtali	53,400	_____
			Total:	603,550	_____

Your Daily Walk

After multiplying from a family of 70 to a nation of 600,000 fighting men in the space of about 400 years, Israel actually declined in population during the next 40 years. In part, the lack of growth was because of the numerous judgments God sent to discipline Israel's disobedience: 14,700 dead after Korah's rebellion (16:49); 24,000 dead after following Balaam's teaching (25:9).

Is God enlarging or shrinking your sphere of influence? Jabez, an obscure figure in 1 Chronicles 4:10, prayed, "Oh that You would bless me indeed, and enlarge my territory . . . So God granted him what he requested." God delights in blessing obedient children. Talk to Him about an "expanded border" with which you want to be entrusted.

NUMBERS 31-33
PREPARING TO POSSESS THE LAND

♡ **Heart of The Passage:** Numbers 33

The real question is not why some pious, humble, believing people suffer, but why some do not.

 **Overview**

During the final days of his life, Moses is active in at least three roles: commander-in-chief of Israel's army; administrator of the nation's internal affairs; and travel guide, bringing the people to the plains of Moab. The Israelite army, using only a token force of troops, exterminates Midian for its idolatrous influence. Later, Moses must deal with the request by the tribes of Reuben, Gad, and Manasseh that they be allowed to settle east of the Jordan. The section closes with a review of the travel route from Egypt to Moab.

Chapter 31	Chapter 32	Chapter 33
Destruction of Midian	Decision of Reuben and Gad	Description of the Journey
Warfare	Wisdom	Wandering

🚶 **Your Daily Walk**

Numbers 33 is both one of the darkest and one of the brightest chapters in the Bible. It is a dark chapter because it chronicles the journey from Egypt to Moab—a journey that should have taken weeks, but instead consumed four decades plus the lives of an entire generation.

But the picture is not all dark, for chapter 33 also portrays the nation's movement under the watchful eye of God. Guided through barren wilderness, provided with manna from heaven, protected from marauding bands, the people experienced God's tender care daily, even as they felt the sting of His discipline.

Christian, do you view God's discipline in your life as "pain with a purpose"? God loves you too much to allow your disobedience to go unpunished. Having read chapter 33, write these words in the margin of your Bible: "A chapter that should have read differently."

A chapter is being written in your life today. How will it read? Learn a lesson from Israel's mistake: take God at His word.

🔍 **Insight:** The End . . . of Balaam, That Is!

Israel's conquest of Midian included the execution of Balaam (31:8). This judgment may seem unduly harsh for the one who had blessed the nation, until it is learned that Balaam masterminded the scheme to defile the Israelites with Midianite women (31:16).

NUMBERS 34-36
INSTRUCTIONS FOR ENTERING THE LAND

♡ Heart of The Passage: Numbers 34:1-15

We cannot rely on God's promises without obeying His commands.

📖 Overview

The book of Numbers closes with a list of the geographic boundaries of the Promised Land and the names of those who will apportion the land to the nine-and-a-half tribes still awaiting the inheritance. Since the Levites are allotted no land, they are given 48 cities scattered throughout Canaan. Laws are established to provide for justice in cases of manslaughter and to protect the inheritance of families who have no surviving male heir.

Chapter 34	Chapter 35	Chapter 36
Borders of the Land	Cities of Refuge	Laws of Inheritance
Geographic Boundaries	Legal Boundaries	

🚶 Your Daily Walk

You cannot enjoy what you do not possess. God had promised to give His people a great land. You'll find the description of its borders in chapter 34.

It extended as far north as Mount Hor and Hamath, as far south as Kadesh-barnea and the river of Egypt (Wadi el-Arish), and as far east as the Jordan River. Sadly, Israel would seldom enjoy the full extent of these promised boundaries. Only briefly in the reigns of David and Solomon would the nation encompass that much territory.

Was God's promise no good? Or was there something else that kept the people from enjoying the full blessing God intended? Every promise has two parts: the promise itself, and the possession of that promise by the person for whom it is intended. God told His nation repeatedly, "Go in and possess the land. It's all yours!" But because of unbelief and indifference, the people settled for God's second best. They could not enjoy what they did not possess.

Thumb back through the *Daily Walk* sections you've already read this month. Is there a promise you've yet to possess—a blessing from God you've yet to stake your claim to? What are you waiting for?

🔍 Insight: Obscure Names, Outstanding Truths

Of those selected by God to allot the land (34:16-29), only Caleb is familiar. But consider the names of others: Shemuel, "name of God"; Elidad, "God has loved"; Hanniel, "favor of God"; Elizaphan, "my God protects"; Paltiel, "God is my deliverance"; Pedahel, "God has redeemed." Names can carry timeless truths, can't they?

DEUTERONOMY 1-4
MOTIVES FOR OBEDIENCE

♡ **Heart of The Passage:** Deuteronomy 1, 4

It requires great listening as well as great preaching to make a great sermon.

📖 **Overview**

In his first of three sermons to the nation, Moses begins with a review of the past. God had promised His people a new homeland, but Israel failed to possess it because of unbelief and disobedience. For 40 years they had wandered and died. Now, with the passing of that unbelieving generation, God has led the nation in smashing victories over Sihon and Og, bringing them to the threshold of the Promised Land once again. But before they are ready to enter, they must learn a crucial lesson from the past—the lesson that obedience brings victory and blessing, while disobedience results only in defeat and judgment.

Chapter 1	Chapters 2-3	Chapter 4
Israel's Past Failure	God's Persistent Faithfulness	Israel's Promising Future
Example	Encouragement	Exhortation

🚶 **Your Daily Walk**

Preaching at its finest involves godly persuasion. When you listen to a preacher, you will often hear him make three painfully pointed statements: (1) "God says to do this: _____." (2) "You are doing this: _____." (3) "Therefore, you need to change _____ now." That's why preaching can make you uncomfortable. It shows you from God's Word where you are wrong and tries to persuade you to change your attitudes or actions to conform with God's commands.

Moses' first sermon to Israel is a masterpiece of godly persuasion as he points out to the people the past, present, and future dealings of God. Israel should obey God because of her past experience of God's deliverance, provision, and judgment; Israel should obey God because of her present experience of God's sufficiency in supplying her needs and in fighting her battles; and Israel should obey God because of her future promises of blessing or cursing, all hinging on her proper response to God's pointed commands.

If you were preaching Deuteronomy 1-4 instead of Moses, which of God's past, present, or future dealings in your life could you point to as proof positive that God ought to be obeyed?

🔍 **Insight:** Standing on the Promises of Old

Moses' confidence in God is largely rooted in God's promises to Israel's forefathers. The phrase "the LORD swore" (1:8) or its equivalent is repeated at least 10 times in Moses' three sermons.

MEASURES OF OBEDIENCE

 Heart of The Passage: Deuteronomy 7

Most of modern man's troubles stem from too much time on his hands and not enough on his knees.

 Overview

Moses' second sermon begins in chapter 5 and extends through chapter 26. He opens with a repetition of the Ten Commandments (hence the name Deuteronomy—"second law") and exhorts the people to obey the LORD from a heart of love, to teach their children obedience, and to be careful not to forget the LORD in times of prosperity. Victory over the pagan occupants of Canaan is assured as long as the people faithfully obey God's commands. They will prevail, not because of their strength, but because of their all-conquering God.

CHAPTER 5	CHAPTER 6	CHAPTER 7
Old Law for a New Generation	New Law for a New Generation	New Hope for a New Generation
TEN COMMANDMENTS	GREATEST COMMAND	FUTURE CONQUEST

 Your Daily Walk

Reading today's section, you may be reminded of the fairy tale about the goose that laid the golden egg. A farmer, upon discovering a most remarkable golden-egg-laying goose, got impatient about having to wait for the daily quota of eggs. He chopped off the goose's head to find the source of the eggs . . . and in a fit of impatience destroyed the very source of his prosperity.

"I want it all—and I want it now!" is the cry of the day, even among many Christians. But God is not limited by our impatient timetables. He gave the Israelites a principle for conquest which still applies today: "little by little" (7:22). God's methods often take time. He could have given the land to Israel in a day, but instead He instructed them to move step by step, trusting Him each "cubit" of the way.

Where are you hoping for instant results in your Christian life: victory over a habit, knowledge of God's Word, spiritual maturity? God's way is not rush, rush, rush but little by little. Look for a small but significant step of growth you can take today: a verse to memorize, a command to obey, a promise to treasure.

Q Insight: Rich Milk and Sticky Fingers

The description of the Promised Land as "the land flowing with milk and honey" pictures it as a land of prosperity and abundance. Milk was part of the Hebrews' staple diet, and so a rich supply of milk indicated vast pasturelands. Honey was considered a delicacy.

DEUTERONOMY 8-11
MENTALITY OF OBEDIENCE

♡ Heart of The Passage: Deuteronomy 8-9

How happy a person is depends upon the depth of his gratitude.

📖 Overview

Moses continues his review of Israel's history as an illustration to the people of God's faithfulness throughout their 40-year wilderness trek. God's provision in the past provides confidence for the future. He will continue to do great things for His people if they continue to walk in obedience to Him. But if they are disobedient, ignore His commands, and worship other gods, God will judge their rebellion. The facts are clear: If Israel loves and obeys God, she will experience blessing. If she disobeys, God's judgment will be sure.

Chapter 8	Chapter 9	Chapters 10-11
Remember God's Goodness	Remember the Golden Calf	Remember to Obey
Reminders from the Past		Responsibilities for the Future

🚶 Your Daily Walk

Spend a few minutes walking through the rooms of your house and noting all the items you own that you did not purchase yourself, but received as gifts. As you look at each item, try to remember who gave it to you and when. If you are like most people, you'll have a difficult time with the assignment.

Moses' review of Israel's history was a verbal recollection of all the good things Israel possessed as a result of God's blessing. The manna in the wilderness and God's other provisions merely foreshadowed what lay ahead: a land flowing with milk and honey. But the promise of prosperity in Canaan pointed to a potential problem. The people of future generations might forget who gave them these good gifts, and take personal credit for their own prosperity. Moses drove home the message that the Israelites were never to forget it was God who supplied their needs and gave them their abundance.

Have you forgotten who gave you the gifts you possess? Write a thank-you note to God, expressing your gratitude for something He has given you in recent days. He loves to hear you say, "Thanks."

🔍 Insight: "Do Not Forget"

Moses reminds his people not to make God's goodness a basis for personal pride. Complete these important thoughts:

Remember how the LORD _____ (8:2).

Remember that God gives you _____ (8:18).

Don't forget how you _____ (9:7).

DEUTERONOMY 12-16
CEREMONIAL REGULATIONS

♡ **Heart of The Passage:** Deuteronomy 12:1-16; 14:22-15:11

When it comes to giving, some people stop at nothing.

📖 Overview

Following his review of the past and preview of the future, Moses turns to the more specific and detailed statutes which will be in effect as Israel takes up residence in the land. Desiring that His people be separate from the nations around them, God commands that Israel's religious life be free from all associations with idolatry. God's chosen people must be characterized by only the highest standards of purity, hygiene, and treatment of the poor—actions which will demonstrate Israel's unique relationship with God. In addition, Israel's feasts must be times of consecration as well as celebration.

Chapter 12	Chapter 13	Chapter 14	Chapter 15	Chapter 16
R E L I G I O U S L A W S C O N C E R N I N G . . .				
Food	Idols	Animals	Debts	Feasts
Regulations Designed to Demonstrate Israel's Uniqueness				

🚶 Your Daily Walk

Are you a grudging or a generous giver? When you hear of some need, do you look for an avenue of giving or an excuse for not giving?

Yesterday you learned that everything you own is a gift from God's hand. Today there is a companion lesson: God expects those whom He has blessed to reflect the same generosity He has shown to them. God specified to Israel that they were to be openhanded with their possessions if they saw a brother or sister in need. Since God was the source of their supply, it was almost as if He were doing the giving Himself. Therefore His people could give generously, knowing their needs would also be met by the Giver of every good gift.

When seen in the light of Christ's command, "Freely you have received, freely give" (Matthew 10:8), your giving can take on new depth and meaning. You can be a source of blessing to someone else, and at the same time receive a blessing yourself. Tap into God's vast storehouse and help someone you know who needs financial assistance this week. Remember, "freely received, freely give."

🔍 Insight: A Painful (and Prohibited) Funeral Ritual (14:1)

The practices of self-inflicted wounds and baldness were signs of mourning for the dead which the Canaanites used as part of their pagan worship. God strictly forbade such activities for His consecrated people. Does He expect any less from you? (See 1 Peter 2:9.)

Heart of The Passage: Deuteronomy 17

If someone calls you "forthright," be careful; he may mean you're right a fourth of the time.

 **Overview**

In addition to the religious laws regulating national worship, Moses sets forth civil laws to govern the selection and application of civil authority in the land. How do you choose a king? How do you prove the trustworthiness of a prophet? How do you protect innocent manslayers? How do you treat captured people humanely and impartially? You'll find the answers in today's section, along with a collection of regulations for prophets and priests, kings and kingdoms.

Chapter 17	Chapter 18	Chapter 19	Chapter 20
Choosing a King	Proving a Prophet	Providing a Refuge	Providing for Peace
Civil Laws		Humanitarian Laws	

 Your Daily Walk

If it is indeed true that "righteousness exalts a nation, but sin is a reproach to any people" (Proverbs 14:34), how would you grade your nation in its efforts to promote righteousness in the following areas (A = Excellent, C = Average, etc.)?

* Dealing with idolatry (objects of worship other than God, 17:2-5)

* Promoting justice (impartiality and fairness, 17:8-11)

* Prohibiting occult practices (witchcraft, horoscopes, 18:9-14)

* Practicing truthfulness (in government, in the courts, 19:15-19)

As a concerned Christian, you cannot do everything to promote national righteousness, but you can do something. Prayer, fasting, phone calls, emails, a fresh commitment to Christian principles—all are powerful deterrents to evil in your nation, but only if you use them. Will you pick one and put it to work today?

Insight: Three Don'ts, One Do for Future Kings

In 17:14-20 you'll find four specific commands directed to future monarchs who would reign over God's people. Complete each command, and compare the performance of Solomon (one such future monarch) as recorded in the book of 1 Kings.

God's Command (Deuteronomy)	Solomon's Response (1 Kings)
"Don't multiply _____" (17:16).	_____ (4:26).
"Don't multiply _____" (17:17).	_____ (11:3).
"Don't multiply _____" (17:17).	_____ (10:14).
"Do make _____" (17:18).	_____ (11:11).

DAILY DEVOTIONS

DEUTERONOMY 21-26
SOCIETAL REGULATIONS

 Heart of The Passage: Deuteronomy 23:1-8; 26:16-19

Cleanliness is next to godliness; but for some, it is next to impossible.

 Overview

How do you promote peace and stability in the land and at the same time deal with unsolved murders, foreign settlers, divorce, family inheritance, stray livestock, sanitation problems, territorial disputes, and a host of other matters? Moses seeks to answer many of these "What if?" situations before they arise in order to ensure the orderly management of God's holy people in the Holy Land.

Chapters 21-22	Chapters 23-24	Chapters 25-26
Holiness in the Home	Holiness Toward the Helpless	Holiness in Human Relations
Domestic Laws	Humane Laws	Societal Laws

 Your Daily Walk

Have you ever seen a restaurant sign that says, "No bare feet allowed"? What was the reason behind that prohibition? Why would restaurants pick on people with bare feet?

Under the Mosaic Law, some people were excluded from the assembly: those with certain defects, those born illegitimately, those of Ammonite or Moabite descent (23:1-3). Why this seemingly arbitrary exclusion of parties from Israel's religious community? Just like the bare feet in the restaurant, each represented a potential source of defilement for all the others in the community.

Mutilation of the body, brazen immorality, and pagan intermarriage were common practices in the Canaanite community. If these defilements were to be kept out of the Israelite camp, certain exclusions had to be enforced.

The church today is often both inclusive and exclusive. Carefully and thoughtfully read Ephesians 2:1-7. Then write down your answer to this question: "Because of my inclusion in the body of Christ, what is one source of defilement I need to exclude from my life of service to God?"

Ask God to give you the strength you need to completely eliminate that sin from your life.

🔍 **Insight:** Buried Like a Common Criminal

The burial of a criminal who is crucified (21:22-23) foreshadows the ignominious death suffered by our LORD. In the New Testament, verse 23 is quoted in reference to Christ's taking the curse of our sins upon Himself: "Cursed is everyone who hangs on a tree" (Galatians 3:13). Also see John 19:31.

DAILY DEVOTIONS

DEUTERONOMY 27-30
COMMITMENT TO THE COVENANT

 Heart of The Passage: Deuteronomy 27-28

We make our decisions, and then our decisions turn around and make us.

 Overview

Moses has come to a solemn, climactic moment in his address to the nation—the time for a recommitment of the people to the covenant. He reminds the new wilderness generation that the potential for God's richest blessing awaits them in the land, as well as the potential for His severest judgment. It all depends on their submissive response to the demands of the covenant. Dramatically Moses delivers the challenge: "I have set before you life and death . . . choose life."

Chapter 27	Chapter 28	Chapter 29	Chapter 30
Prescribed Ceremonies	Promised Blessings	Conditions of the Covenant	Commitment of the Nation
The Covenant Reviewed		The Covenant Renewed	

 Your Daily Walk

"I wish I were dead!" Perhaps at an unguarded moment of despair or shame, you vented your frustration with such words. But you didn't really mean them literally. Most people want to live. In fact, they will do just about anything to preserve their life. But that strong survival instinct doesn't always carry over into the spiritual realm.

Moses made the choice transparently clear for Israel with these two simple (and unalterable) formulas:

OBEDIENCE = LIFE

DISOBEDIENCE = DEATH

And yet, in the months ahead you will read the tragic national consequences of Israel's decisions.

You are facing similar decisions today with equally far-reaching consequences. You, like Israel, can choose death by rebelling against God's will. Or by obeying you can choose life and daily fellowship with the God of life. Which will it be?

Take a note card and write the two formulas on it. Tape the card to your refrigerator, bathroom mirror, or dashboard. Let it remind you often of God's timeless principle of life and death. The choice is yours.

 Insight: The Day the Slave Markets Were Glutted

The horrible curse of 28:68 literally came true! After the fall of Jerusalem in A.D. 70, the slave markets of Egypt became so glutted with captive Israelites that there were not enough buyers for them all. God always keeps His promises—those that carry blessing and those that carry punishment.

DEUTERONOMY 31-34
CULMINATION OF MOSES' MINISTRY

♡ **Heart of The Passage:** Deuteronomy 32, 34

When the wind is at your back, be sure to remember God.

📖 Overview

With the covenant reestablished and the nation poised at the Jordan River, Moses completes his duties as leader of God's people. He commissions Joshua as his successor with a sober warning of Israel's future rebellion. In order for the people to remember his message of life, Moses records his final words as a song and teaches the melody and message to the nation. After pronouncing blessings on each of the 12 tribes, Moses climbs Mount Nebo for a final glimpse of the Promised Land. There he dies, physically strong in spite of his 120 years. And though his final resting place remains a mystery to this day, he had the finest of Undertakers to arrange his funeral.

CHAPTER 31	CHAPTER 32	CHAPTER 33	CHAPTER 34
Moses' Successor	Moses' Song	Moses' Blessing	God's Benediction
THE FINAL DAYS OF MOSES			

🚶 Your Daily Walk

You've heard of fair-weather friends—the kind who flock to you when everything is going right, and disappear when things start going wrong. But have you ever heard of "foul-weather friends," the kind who cling to you when things are going badly, and ignore you when everything is running smoothly?

"Foul-weather friends" is a perfect description of the children of Israel. During their times of need in the wilderness, Israel followed after God despite occasional grumblings and rebellions. But God warned the nation that coming prosperity would bring indifference toward Him. When the Promised Land was conquered and occupied, the nation would abandon God for idols (31:16; 32:15, 18).

When you're face-to-face with a crisis, it's natural to cry out to God for help. But what about when things are running smoothly? When the wind is at your back, your health is excellent, there's money in the checkbook and the bills are all paid—what then? Try singing a few verses from the "Song of Moses" (chapter 32), expressing your devotion to God in the good times as well as the bad.

🔍 Insight: A Fitting Epitaph for Moses' Tombstone

"The eternal God is your refuge, and underneath are the everlasting arms" (33:27).

A new churchwide Bible adventure
from Walk Thru the Bible!

God's **Grand** Story *His Word. Your Life.*

A six-week campaign designed to engage the entire congregation in developing a lifelong habit of living God's Word every day.

Campaign Includes:

- Sermon topics & outlines
- Individual daily Bible readings
- Group DVD Bible study
- Dynamic live event campaign kick off

With God's Grand Story, you just became the pastor's best friend!

—Kurt Parker, Senior Pastor, Harborside Church, Safety Harbor, FL.

FREE
GOD'S GRAND STORY PARTICIPANT'S GUIDEBOOK EXCERPT

Learn more about this easy to implement, momentum-building campaign at **www.walkthru.org/ggs**.

THE
Keyword Learning System™
learn the major **themes** of the Bible

Eye-catching graphics provide an **innovative** and **fun** way to learn the **"big ideas"** of the Bible! The visuals are filled with lots of **hidden keys** that help unlock the themes of the Old and New Testament.

Keyword Learning System™ includes the *OT39 Old Testament* and *NT27 New Testament* series:

- Bible Flashcards
- Bible Flashcards App for iPad and iPhone
- Coloring Books
- Slideshow Presentation for PowerPoint and Keynote
  Each component sold separately

View the Complete System at **www.keywordvisuals.com**